PROFESSIONAL COOKERY

Bryan Marsh

Chairman of the Food Services Department
Don Head Secondary School
Richmond Hill, Ontario

McGraw-Hill Ryerson Limited

Toronto Montreal New York Auckland Bogotá Cairo Guatemala
Hamburg Johannesburg Lisbon London Madrid Mexico New Delhi
Panama Paris San Juan São Paulo Singapore Sydney Tokyo

PROFESSIONAL COOKERY

Copyright © McGraw-Hill Ryerson Ltd., 1985

ISBN 0-07-548641-5

1 2 3 4 5 6 7 8 9 0 D 4 3 2 1 0 9 8 7 6 5

Printed and bound in Canada by John Deyell Company

Canadian Cataloguing in Publication Data

Marsh, Bryan, date
    Professional Cookery

Includes index.

ISBN 0-07-548641-5

1. Food service – Canada   I. Title
TX943.M37 1985   641.5 '7   C84-099653-5

ACKNOWLEDGEMENTS

This text could not have been completed without the assistance of co-workers Willi Boedefeld, John Bradbury and Aussie Topping, who provided valuable input and constructive criticism. My thanks to Don Lipsett and Jennifer Joiner of McGraw-Hill Ryerson for their patience and encouragement throughout the project. To Susan Steckel, who typed most of the manuscript, I am greatly indebted for her constant support, patience, encouragement and understanding.

B.M.

TABLE OF CONTENTS

PROFESSIONAL COOKERY

CHAPTER 1
THE FOOD SERVICE INDUSTRY

The aim of this book is to provide you with basic training in the field of professional cookery. You will also learn about employment opportunities in the rapidly growing food industry. The food industry is one of the fastest growing industries in North America. More people eat at least one meal away from home every day than ever before. Our changing society, in which increasing numbers of women are employed outside the home, is faced with a greater demand for dining-out facilities. This means there are more employment opportunities available in the preparation of food. You can find food industry jobs in a wide variety of facilities, including institutions, large cafeterias, private clubs, airline kitchens, large hotels, specialty restaurants, coffee shops, drive-ins and a large number of chain and franchised restaurants.

A career in the field of professional cookery depends largely on your desire and ambition. The following is a list of some of the positions that exist within this field. Depending on the size of the food establishment, two or more of these positions may be combined to form one position.

Executive chef or chef This person is in full charge of the kitchen and its staff. He or she is responsible for menu planning and the coordination of all work in the kitchen.
Sous chef He or she is second in command in the kitchen.
Chef steward This chef has the added responsibility of purchasing food supplies. This position is usually found in medium-sized kitchens.
Working chef This person is usually in charge of kitchens in smaller hotels and restaurants, where the kitchen staff is not large. During production, the working chef both supervises and cooks.
Night chef He or she takes over the responsibility for the kitchen when the executive chef and the sous chef have left for the day.

Banquet chef This person is responsible for all the food prepared for banquets and parties.

Second cook or soup cook The responsibility here is to produce all stocks, soups and sauces. In addition, the soup cook may prepare all stewed, braised and sautéed food.

Roast cook or broiler cook Depending on the size of the kitchen, this may be one or two positions. The roast cook is responsible for the preparation of all roasts and gravies which accompany the roasts. The broiler cook is responsible for all broiled foods.

Vegetable cook This person is responsible for the preparation and cooking of all vegetables.

A professional cook (Courtesy of David Portigal & Co.)

Fry cook He or she is responsible for the preparation of all fried items such as eggs, omelets, fritters, croquettes and potatoes.

Swing cook This person relieves other cooks on their days off. This involves covering a different station each day. Therefore, this job requires thorough knowledge, skill and experience.

Garde manger He or she is in charge of all cold preparations in the kitchen. This includes cold meats, salads, sandwiches, dressings, cold sauces, canapés and cold hors-d'oeuvres.

Pastry chef This person supervises the work in the pastry department. Included in the duties are dessert menu planning, cake decoration and the preparation of sweet table ornamental pieces.

Assistant pastry chef He or she is responsible to the pastry chef for the production of all items found on the dessert menu, such as cakes, pies, French pastries and puddings.

Baker This person is responsible for the production of all breads, rolls and muffins.

Other jobs found in larger kitchens include pantry worker, salad maker, sandwich maker, cook's helper and baker's helper. As you can see, there is indeed a wide variety of opportunities within the field of professional cookery.

Working in a kitchen is a demanding job and one that you must be prepared to dedicate yourself to if you are to be successful. Success does not come easily. To achieve it, you should have or develop the following characteristics:

1. a willingness to work
2. the ability to take direction and criticism
3. the ability to cooperate with other workers
4. good personal cleanliness
5. good health
6. interest in your work
7. dependability
8. initiative
9. persistence

The cornerstone of good food preparation is the use of sound basic recipes and one's own creativity and imagination. Bookstores have many shelves full of excellent cookbooks with a multitude of recipes both at the domestic and professional level. As a result, this book is not intended to provide a vast collection of recipes. Those recipes that do appear here are included to illustrate the various cooking methods and preparation techniques discussed in the book.

CHAPTER 2
KITCHEN SAFETY

Watch for These Words

implication   cleaver   grounded

responsibility   ensure   yank

promote   conduct   regulations

pry   smother   flash

particle   aisle   extinguish

grate   recurring   ventilation

How to Use These Words

1. The extension cord which stretched across the __XXXX__ between the shelves caused the cook to trip.
2. Safety __XXXX__ must be followed by all employees.
3. Accidents often have serious __XXXX__.
4. When you are using a __XXXX__, be careful of bone splinters.
5. Copper or aluminium wire is used to __XXXX__ electricity.
6. The cook tried to __XXXX__ the lid off with a knife.
7. Poor __XXXX__ of gas appliances can cause explosions.
8. It is the __XXXX__ of all employees to practise safe working habits.
9. __XXXX__ backache can be caused by incorrect lifting methods.
10. The apprentice was asked to __XXXX__ some cheddar cheese.
11. When you __XXXX__ a fire, you cut off the supply of oxygen to the fire.
12. Small __XXXX__ of broken glass can cause nasty cuts.
13. If you __XXXX__ the electrical cord, it may break.
14. Fat that is too hot often causes a __XXXX__ fire.

15. To __XXXX__ safe working conditions, all safety rules must be followed.
16. Improperly __XXXX__ electrical equipment is a safety hazard.
17. Water will not __XXXX__ a fat fire.
18. Awareness of potential hazards will __XXXX__ safe working conditions.

People working in commercial kitchens are exposed to a wide variety of accidents. These range from simple strains to severe cuts and burns. Most accidents are the direct result of carelessness. Employees do not always pay attention to what they are doing and accidents occur. If a serious accident occurs, the **implications** of the injury are two-fold. The employee loses time from the job, suffering physically and financially, and the employer loses the services of the employee. It is the **responsibility** of all food service employees to constantly practise safe working habits and to **promote** these safe practices with their fellow workers.

To ensure these safe working habits and practices, it is necessary to remember some common-sense rules.

AVOIDING CUTS

Cuts normally are the result of improper use of knives or of using the wrong knife for the task.
1. Use the correct knife for the job.
2. Use sharp knives. A dull knife is more dangerous because it may slip off the food you are trying to cut.
3. Use a cutting board. Never cut on a metal surface.
4. Don't slice food in your hand.
5. Always cut in a direction away from your body.
6. Don't use knives to open cans or to **pry** off lids.
7. Never try to catch a falling knife. Stand back and let it fall.
8. Always carry a knife by your side with the tip pointing down.
9. Pick knives up by the handle, and be sure to keep handles free of grease or other slippery materials.
10. Never leave knives in soapy dishwater. Someone else may reach into the sink and grasp a knife by the blade.
11. When slicing round foods such as onions or carrots, cut a flat base so that the food will sit firmly and not shift when it is being cut.
12. When wiping or cleaning a knife, clean it from the back edge. Sharp knives will easily cut through towels.

implication—involvement

responsibility—the state of being accountable for
promote—encourage

pry—move by a levering action

13. Always store knives in the racks or slots provided for them. Do not store knives in a drawer.
14. Large pieces of broken glass should be swept up by using a broom and dust pan. Small **particles** should be picked up with a damp paper towel.
15. When **grating** food, don't **grate** too close to the grating surface.
16. Foods to be chopped with a **cleaver** must be set firmly so as not to slip or jump.
17. Don't force foods through a meat saw. Gentle pressure will **ensure** that the blade does not snap or jump from the bone.
18. Always use the guard provided when you are operating the slicing machine.
19. Before cleaning power slicers or meat saws, always disconnect the power cord.

particle—a tiny piece

grate—shred by rubbing on a rough surface

cleaver—a heavy knife used for chopping through bone

ensure—make sure of

AVOIDING BURNS

Burns are generally the result of inattentiveness. They can be extremely painful and slow to heal.

1. Always use pot holders or dry towels to handle hot pots. Wet towels will **conduct** heat more rapidly than dry towels.
2. Pots on the stove should have their handles turned in so that people walking by will not upset them. However, make sure the handles are not in contact with open flames.
3. When taking the lid off a hot pot, tilt the lid away from you to avoid steam burns.
4. When checking or removing food from a hot oven, pull the oven rack out. This protects the back of your hands from burns.
5. Wear close fitting clothes. Loose clothing may catch on pot handles or come in contact with open flames.
6. Always warn other workers (particularly dishwashers) about hot pans.
7. Food to be deep fried should be dry and at room temperature. Wet, cold food causes spattering when lowered into hot fat.
8. Don't drop food items into hot fat. Gently lower them into the fat to avoid spattering and burns.
9. Don't overfill hot food containers.
10. Always **smother** fat fires: do not throw water on them. Burning fat floats on water and spreads rapidly.
11. Know the location of fire extinguishers and fire blankets.

conduct—transmit or convey; carry

smother—cover so as to cut off the air supply

AVOIDING FALLS

Falls are usually the result of carelessness on someone's part. Slippery lettuce leaves or liquid spills which have not been promptly cleaned up are particularly dangerous.

1. Keep floors clean and dry. Clean up all spills immediately.
2. Walk, don't run, in the kitchen.
3. Keep all work areas and **aisles** clear of wagons, crates, chairs and electrical cords.
4. Use a proper step ladder in storerooms. Don't use tables or chairs to stand on.
5. Always pay attention to where you are going.
6. Replace torn mats on the floor as soon as they are discovered.

aisle—a passageway

Mop spills up right away.

Spilled liquids can cause major accidents in the kitchen.

AVOIDING STRAINS

Strains are caused by using the incorrect method of lifting. They usually occur in the back and often lead to **recurring** back problems.

recurring—happening again and again

1. Don't try to carry loads which are too heavy for you. If you need help, ask for it.
2. Lift loads with your leg muscles rather than with your back muscles.
3. Always step carefully when moving heavy loads.
4. Store heavy items on bottom shelves.

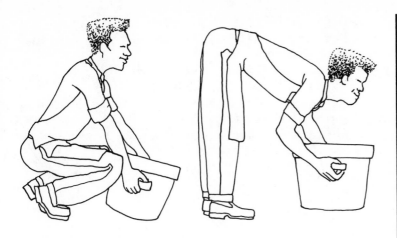

AVOIDING SHOCKS

Shocks result from touching exposed electrical wiring or from operating improperly **grounded** electrical equipment. Severe electrical shock can cause death.

1. All electrical equipment should be grounded.
2. Electrical cords should be checked regularly to ensure that they are in good repair.
3. Remove cords from the power source by the plug. Don't **yank** on the cord.
4. Don't handle electrical equipment with wet hands or while you are standing in water.
5. Check that equipment is turned off before plugging it into the power source.
6. Always unplug electrical appliances before washing them.

grounded—electrical conductor is connected to the ground and shock is carried to the ground

yank—pull or jerk suddenly

Don't yank on electrical cords.

AVOIDING FIRES

Fires need not occur if proper attention is paid to safety **regulations**. You should always be familiar with the location of extinguishers and with the operation of each type of extinguisher.

regulations—rules

flash—sudden burst of flame

extinguish—put out

1. Don't overheat fat. This can lead to a **flash** fire.
2. Don't overfill fryers. They should be no more than two-thirds full.
3. Hot fat should never be left unattended.
4. Wipe up fat spills immediately.
5. Never use water to **extinguish** a fat fire. This simply spreads the fat and the fire.
6. Always smother fat fires with any of the following:
     chemical extinguisher
     fibreglass fire blanket
     damp towel
     pot cover
     baking soda
     salt

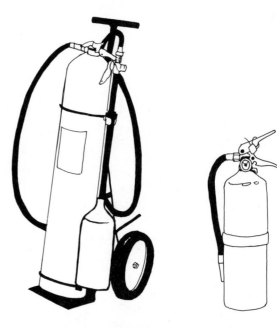

7. Know the location of fire extinguishers.
8. Remember that gas needs **ventilation**.
9. In case of fire, don't panic. Remain calm and follow the required procedures.

ventilation—access to air

Always be alert to **potentially hazardous** situations. **Anticipate** and act. Don't leave it for someone else to do. Remember that all accidents, no matter how minor, should be reported to your supervisor immediately.

potentially—possibly
hazardous—dangerous
anticipate—expect or foresee

Find the Answers to These Questions

1. What is the main cause of accidents?
2. Why should you not leave knives in soapy dishwater?
3. How should you clean a knife?
4. A knife is falling. What should you do?
5. Before you clean power equipment, what precaution should you take?
6. What precautions should you take with pots on a stove?
7. Why do you not use water to extinguish a fat fire?
8. Explain the procedure for extinguishing a fat fire.
9. Explain the proper method of lifting heavy objects.
10. What precautions should be taken before food is deep fried?
11. What does "properly grounded" mean?
12. What do you need to know about fire extinguishers?

CHAPTER 3
SANITATION AND HYGIENE

Watch for These Words

adhere
contaminate
inevitable
environment
microorganism
beneficial
essential

process
susceptible
dormant
sewage
emerge
insecticide
receptacle

administer
maintenance
lodged
porous
intestines

How to Use These Words

1. Effective sanitation is a __XXXX__ which involves all kitchen staff.
2. When food is frozen, any bacteria present are __XXXX__ but not dead.
3. Customers often return to a restaurant because they feel safe in its clean __XXXX__.
4. One way of eliminating roaches is by using a strong __XXXX__.
5. Human waste passes through the __XXXX__ before it is eliminated.
6. A pest control expert __XXXX__ insecticides to control roaches.
7. The __XXXX__ conditions for bacterial growth are food, warmth and moisture.
8. It is __XXXX__ that unsanitary kitchen conditions will lead to food poisoning.
9. It is important to __XXXX__ to all the rules of sanitation.
10. Mice __XXXX__ from their nests at night.
11. Eggs and egg products are __XXXX__ to bacterial contamination.
12. The customer had a food particle __XXXX__ in his teeth.
13. Some bacteria are very __XXXX__ to human beings.

14. Garbage ___XXXX___ should be tightly covered.
15. Water soaked into the material because it was ___XXXX___.
16. The caretaker was responsible for the ___XXXX___ of the kitchen.
17. Germs are also known as ___XXXX___.
18. Workers who do not wash their hands after using the toilet may ___XXXX___ the food.
19. Some insects feed on garbage and ___XXXX___.

BACTERIA

Sanitation in food service is the science and practice of maintaining generally healthy conditions for food preparation. If this practice is not **adhered** to by all members of the staff, food **contamination**, food poisoning and the loss of business are the **inevitable** results.

To understand the nature of sanitary conditions, we must become aware of the conditions which lead to an unsanitary **environment**. The most common source of food contamination is **microorganisms** known as bacteria. Bacteria are present everywhere. Some are **beneficial**, while others are harmful to our health. Beneficial bacteria are used in the production of cheese, yogurt and buttermilk. However, harmful bacteria can cause illness, infection and sometimes death.

All bacteria have three **essential** conditions for growth. These are food, warmth and moisture. Once these conditions exist, harmful bacteria grow and multiply at an alarming rate. In their growth, bacteria divide in two. These two produce four and so on. So in the space of a few hours, the bacteria will have multiplied tremendously. This growth is a fast and continuous **process**. To control the growth of bacteria, it is necessary to eliminate or at least minimize the conditions for growth.

When they multiply, bacteria produce toxins. These are the poisons which contaminate food and cause sickness. With some bacteria, the toxins are not produced until after the food is consumed. This makes it difficult to detect contaminated food. With other bacteria, the toxins are produced before the food is consumed. Usually spoilage can be detected from the odour or the appearance of the food.

Food

Some foods are more **susceptible** to bacterial spoilage than others. Extra care must be taken with the following foods to prevent them from becoming contaminated:

adhere—give support to
contamination—spoilage
inevitable—sure to happen

environment—surrounding area
microorganism—organism of microscopic size; germs, bacteria
beneficial—helpful

essential—necessary

process—series of changes

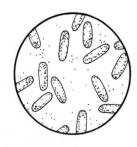

susceptible—capable of being affected

1. Soups, stocks, sauces and gravies
2. Meat and meat products, particularly ground meats
3. Milk and milk products
4. Eggs and egg products
5. Any foods that are handled
6. Any foods that are reheated

Warmth (Temperature)

Bacteria grow fastest at warm temperatures, between 15°C and 38°C (60°F and 100°F). Below 15°C (60°F) bacteria are less active and become **dormant** as the temperature drops to freezing. Bacteria are not killed by cold. They become less active but will begin to grow again as the temperature gets warmer. When the temperature reaches 4°C (40°F), food is in the danger **zone**. This danger zone continues until the temperature reaches 60°C (140°F). For this reason, refrigerators are kept at temperatures between 1°C (34°F) and 3°C (38°F). Bacteria grow very slowly at these temperatures and food stored in the refrigerator will keep for a long time. To kill bacteria, food must be heated to temperatures above 60°C (140°F) or, if possible, to boiling (100°C or 212°F). To be completely sure, the food should be held at these temperatures for three to five minutes, as some bacteria can withstand boiling temperatures for a short time.

dormant—inactive

zone—a distinct, defined area

Moisture

Bacteria require moisture for growth. Foods such as custards, sauces and creams are ideal for bacterial growth, while dry foods such as sugar and raw rice are not easily contaminated by bacteria.

PESTS

Food may be contaminated by pests such as flies, roaches, rats and mice. The most common insects which contaminate food are flies and roaches. The common fly will eat anything from garbage and **sewage** to food being prepared

sewage—waste matter

for human **consumption**. Unlike the careful food worker, the fly does not wash after feasting on garbage and before

consumption—usage

emerge—come out
insecticide—substance
used to kill insects
receptacle—container
administered—applied

maintenance—keeping in
good condition

detergent—substance used
with water for removing
dirt

thorough—complete

lodged—stuck

porous—capable of
retaining moisture

moving on to the food you are preparing. So the fly contaminates everything it touches.

Roaches like to nest in warm, dark places. They are rarely seen during the day, but they **emerge** at night to feed on food particles. Like the fly, roaches contaminate whatever they touch. Insect pests are controlled by eliminating their breeding places and by the use of **insecticides**. Covered garbage **receptacles** will help to eliminate breeding places. Insecticides should only be **administered** by a reliable pest control company.

Rodents such as rats and mice are carriers of disease and contamination. You can identify their presence in kitchens and storerooms by their tell-tale droppings and by chewed food bags. Rodents multiply rapidly and are extremely difficult to eliminate if they are left unchecked. Traps and poisons are used to control rodents. However, these must be used with care. The best method of control is prevention. Make sure that food in storerooms is kept in tightly sealed metal or plastic containers. Wipe up spills and dropped food scraps immediately. Keep garbage in covered containers. If you eliminate the food supply for rodents, they will not stay around very long.

GOOD SANITATION PRACTICES

Unsanitary conditions will exist if the kitchen and its contents are not kept clean. Regular daily **maintenance** of floors and walls is necessary for effective sanitation. Floors should be swept and washed daily with a strong, hot **detergent**. Walls must be kept free from dust. Any spills or splashes on walls must be washed away with hot detergent.

Kitchen equipment must be kept clean and in good repair to prevent food contamination. The equipment should be designed so that it is both easy to clean and easy to check for **thorough** cleanliness. Kitchen tools and utensils that are not maintained hygienically may cause food poisoning. Some tools such as meat saws, mincers and strainers are particularly susceptible to having food particles **lodged** in them. If care is not taken to make sure these tools are absolutely clean, germs may multiply and contaminate food the next time the tool is used. Another source of potential contamination is cracked or chipped dishes. Once the surface of glazed dishes is broken, the **porous** nature of the material is a natural breeding ground for harmful germs and bacteria. All cracked or chipped dishes should be discarded as soon as they are discovered.

Good sanitation practices (Courtesy of Diversity Corporation. Photo by Herb Nott.)

Dishes, glassware and cutlery can be a source of contamination if they are not properly washed and handled. Most commercial food services are equipped with dishwashing machines which, when properly maintained, effectively sanitize dishes and cutlery. The minimum wash temperature required for safe washing is 60°C (140°F), while the minimum rinse temperature required is 82°C (180°F). Before washing, dishes should be scraped, prerinsed and then placed in the proper dish racks for washing. Cutlery should be soaked in a presoak solution to soften hardened food particles before washing. Glassware should always be washed before other dishes or after the wash water has been changed.

During the final rinse of dishes, the dishwashing machine automatically adds a wetting agent to the rinse water. This wetting agent helps the water to bead on the dishes and virtually eliminates water spots when the dishes air dry.

Clean dishes, glassware and cutlery must be carefully handled and stored to keep them sanitary. Care must be taken not to leave unsightly fingerprints on the clean service ware.

Personal Hygiene

Human beings often spread microorganisms to food. Food workers who do not follow strict rules of personal hygiene are a potential hazard to customers. Sources of food-poisoning bacteria in humans include the **intestines**, nose, throat, cuts and open sores. Bacteria can be spread

intestines—the bowels

by coughing, sneezing and by the hands. Smoking can also aid in the spread of bacteria. When you smoke, the risk of saliva being transferred to your hands and later contaminating food is greater.

Another common unsanitary practice is to use the same spoon for more than one tasting of food that is being prepared. If the spoon is used more than once, germs from the taster's mouth will be **transferred** to the food. Here are some common-sense personal hygiene rules that will help you to become a safe and hygienic food worker.

1. Bathe or shower daily.
2. Wash the hair frequently. Keep it neat and confined in a net or cap when you are working with food.
3. Brush your teeth frequently, particularly after eating.
4. Visit the dentist for regular check-ups.
5. Wear clean uniforms in the kitchen.
6. Hands should be washed after:
   a. using the toilet
   b. sneezing or coughing into your hands
   c. smoking
   d. combing your hair
   e. handling money
   f. blowing your nose
   g. touching your face
   h. eating
   i. handling raw meat, poultry, fish or any unwashed raw food
   j. shaking hands with someone
   k. handling used cutlery
7. Don't work if you have open cuts or sores, a cold, a sore throat or a runny nose.
8. Don't wear nail polish when you are working with food. It may flake or chip and fall into the food.
9. Keep fingernails clean and trimmed.
10. Don't wear jewellery on your hands when you are handling food.

It is important that you look neat and well groomed when you work with food. This **creates** a favourable first impression on customers who may come in contact with you. If your appearance is clean and neat, the customer will have confidence in your workmanship. Here is a grooming check-list to help you **convey** the best possible impression to both customers and fellow employees.

transferred—carried to

creates—causes to exist

convey—pass on

CHECK-LIST OF PERSONAL GROOMING HABITS

Head

hair neatly trimmed and combed
dandruff controlled
hair not greasy
neck and ears clean

Face

teeth clean
clean shaven
no excess make-up

Body

no body odour
freshly bathed or showered
perfume or shaving lotion not too strong

Hands

clean
clean, neatly trimmed fingernails
no excess jewellery

Feet

clean socks or stockings
proper footwear

Posture

erect stance
no rounded, slouched shoulders

Overall Appearance

appropriate, well-fitting clothes
clean, shined shoes
confident look

The practice of effective sanitation and hygiene is an ongoing process. It is the responsibility of all those who work with food to make cleanliness and freedom from contamination a team effort. From dishwasher to executive chef and from bus person to maître d' or hostess, all must be **relentless** in their **pursuit** of a clean, healthy work environment.

relentless—always working at
pursuit—active seeking

Find the Answers to These Questions

1. Why is sanitation so important in the food industry?
2. Name three sources of contamination in food.
3. Bacteria are used in the production of what food products?
4. What are the essential conditions for the growth of bacteria?
5. How do bacteria increase in number?
6. What substances are produced when bacteria are growing?
7. Name six groups of foods that are easily spoiled by bacteria.
8. At what temperature are bacteria destroyed?
9. What is the danger zone?
10. What foods are not easily contaminated by bacteria?
11. How do pests contaminate food?
12. Why should cracked or chipped dishes be discarded?
13. How do humans spread bacteria?
14. Why is it important for the food service worker to look neat and well groomed?
15. Who is responsible for effective sanitation and hygiene?

CHAPTER 4
TOOLS AND EQUIPMENT

Watch for These Words

proficiency	insulated	faucet
encountered	consistently	scorch
implements	countermass	staple
tapers	mallet	caster
paring	uniform	commissary
serrated	canapés	conventional
perforated	gauge	

How to Use These Words

1. Customers often returned to the bakery because the pastries were of __XXXX__ high quality.
2. The veal cutlets were flattened by using a __XXXX__.
3. The chops were burnt because the pan they were cooked in was not made of heavy __XXXX__ metal.
4. These tools are the __XXXX__ that are needed for the job.
5. The __XXXX__ edge of the knife snagged on the customer's sweater.
6. In order to wash her hands, the salad maker had to turn on the __XXXX__.
7. Cream sauces and soups __XXXX__ or burn easily.
8. A French knife __XXXX__ to a point at the tip.
9. After much practice, the student achieved a degree of __XXXX__ with a French knife.
10. The ingredient bin did not roll easily when the cook tried to move it because a __XXXX__ was missing.
11. The cook burned her hand because she did not use an __XXXX__ pot holder.
12. Some students __XXXX__ difficulty when they tried to do recipe costing problems.
13. Following recipes and using accurate measurements ensure __XXXX__ results when cooking.

14. A flight kitchen which supplies food for a number of airlines could be called a __XXXX__.
15. The steamer pan was __XXXX__ with many holes.
16. Rice is a __XXXX__ food of many Asian countries.
17. __XXXX__ ovens cook more slowly than convection ovens.
18. Before dinner the hostess served a tray of delicious __XXXX__.
19. The apprentice cut himself while __XXXX__ the apple.
20. The __XXXX__ balanced the mass of the pan on the other side of the scale.

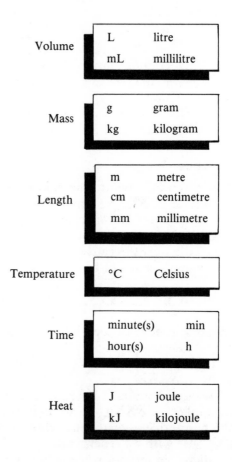

Volume	L	litre
	mL	millilitre
Mass	g	gram
	kg	kilogram
Length	m	metre
	cm	centimetre
	mm	millimetre
Temperature	°C	Celsius
Time	minute(s)	min
	hour(s)	h
Heat	J	joule
	kJ	kilojoule

proficiency—skill

encountered—came in contact with

A thorough knowledge of the tools of the trade and **proficiency** in their use are essential if one is to succeed in the field of professional cookery. The commercial kitchen is filled with tools and equipment, all designed for specific functions. In this chapter you will become familiar with the uses of the most common tools, utensils and equipment **encountered** in the commercial kitchen.

TOOLS

Implements such as serving spoons, knives and wire whisks are constantly used in kitchens.

implements—tools

Cutting Tools

A **French knife** is the most widely used knife in the kitchen. It is used for slicing, chopping, dicing and mincing food. The blade is wide near the handle and **tapers** to a point.

tapers—becomes gradually smaller toward one end

A **boning knife** has a short, thin blade and is used to remove raw meat from the bone with a minimum of waste.

A **butcher knife** has a curved, pointed and heavy blade used to section and slice raw meat.

A **roast beef slicer** has a long, round-ended blade. It is used to slice any size of roast.

A **paring knife** has a short, pointed blade. It is used for **paring** vegetables and fruit.

A **citrus knife** has a short, flexible blade which is **serrated** on both sides. It is used to cut citrus fruits into sections.

paring—peeling
serrated—with fine, teeth-like notches

A **vegetable peeler** is a paring tool with a swivel blade and a cutting edge designed much like a safety razor. It is used to remove a thin layer of skin from vegetables with a minimum of waste.

A **cleaver** has a heavy, wide, rectangular blade which is used to chop through medium bones.

An **oyster knife** has a short, thin, dull-edged blade with a tapered point. It is used to pry open oysters.

A **meat saw** has a fine-toothed blade which is attached to a bow-shaped frame much like a hack saw. It is used to saw through bones.

vegetable peeler

oyster knife

Stirring and Serving Tools

A **wooden spoon** is made of hardwood and is used for stirring, mixing and creaming.

A **solid kitchen spoon** is made of stainless steel and is used for serving, stirring and folding.

A **perforated kitchen spoon** is made of stainless steel **perforated** with holes to allow liquid to pass through. It is used to serve small cooked vegetables such as peas or diced carrots.

perforated—having rows of small holes

A **slotted kitchen spoon** is made of stainless steel with large slots cut in the bowl of the spoon. This spoon is used to serve larger cooked items without the liquids.

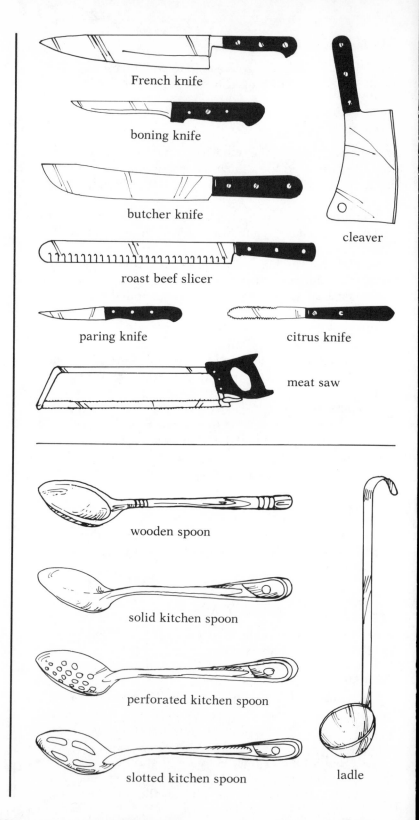

French knife

boning knife

butcher knife

cleaver

roast beef slicer

paring knife

citrus knife

meat saw

wooden spoon

solid kitchen spoon

perforated kitchen spoon

slotted kitchen spoon

ladle

A **ladle** is a long-handled, stainless steel cup. It is used to dip and serve liquids where portion control is necessary. It can also be used to stir and to mix.

Food tongs are usually made of a spring-type stainless steel in a U-shape with saw-toothed grips on each end. They are used for handling food without touching it with the hands.

A **cook's fork** is a two-pronged fork with a handle made of **insulating** material. It is used to hold meats for slicing, to turn roasts and to serve.

food tongs

insulating—will not transfer heat

cook's fork

turner or lifter

A **turner** or **lifter** is made of stainless steel with an off-set, **flexible**, wide blade. It is used to slide under and turn pancakes, fried eggs, hamburgers and other meats on the grill or broiler.

A **wooden paddle** comes in various lengths and is used to stir foods in deep stock pots and steam kettles.

flexible—easily bent

wooden paddle

A **wire whip** or **whisk** is made of a series of thin loops of stainless steel wire with the ends meeting in a handle. It is used for blending, mixing and whipping eggs, batters, sauces, gravies and cream soups.

Measuring Tools

Some of the most important tools in the kitchen are measuring tools. Accurate measurement in following recipes minimizes poor results and ensures **consistently** high food quality.

Measuring spoons are made of stainless steel, aluminium or plastic and are available in 2 mL (½ teaspoon),

wire whip or whisk

consistently—the same as before

portion scales

5 mL (1 teaspoon) and 15 mL (1 tablespoon) sizes. They are used for measuring small amounts of dry and liquid ingredients.

Measuring cups are made of glass, plastic or stainless steel. They are **graduated** in metric and/or imperial measure. These measures are available in sizes ranging from 250 mL (1 cup) to 1 L (4 cups). Measuring cups are used to measure liquids and some dry ingredients.

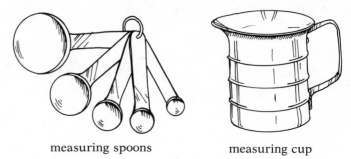

measuring spoons   measuring cup

Portion scales are used for measuring food portions. They have a single platform on which food is placed to calculate its mass. A dial on the front of the scale is graduated in grams to 1 kg.

A **baker's scale** is a very accurate twin-platform scale. One platform contains a scoop on which the material to be measured is placed. On the other platform a **countermass** is placed which has the same mass as the scoop. On the front of the scale there is a bar graduated in grams to 1 kg. The bar has a movable mass attached to it which is placed at the amount one wants to measure. As the material to be measured is added to the scoop, extra kilogram masses are placed on the platform with the countermass. The correct mass is measured when a balance between both platforms is reached.

A **portion scoop** is a bowl of known capacity which is attached to a handle. It has a thumb-controlled, rotating bar inside the bowl which releases the contents. Portion scoops come in a variety of sizes and are used to shape and measure servings of foods such as mashed potatoes, rice and ice cream.

Other Tools

A **skimmer** is like a perforated ladle with a shallow bowl. It is used to skim grease, **scum** and food particles from stocks, soups and sauces.

A **strainer** is a perforated metal bowl with a long handle and a hook so that it can be placed across pots. It is used for straining food.

baker's scales

portion scoop

skimmer

strainer

A **colander** is a perforated bowl with loop handles and feet. It is used for draining washed salad greens, fruits and cooked foods such as pasta.

A **grater** is a hollow metal box with different-sized grids used for grating and shredding foods such as cheese and vegetables.

A **China cap strainer** is a large, cone-shaped metal strainer with a long handle and a hook so that it can be placed across pots. It is used to strain soups, sauces and semi-solids which may be forced through the perforations.

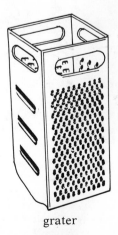

grater

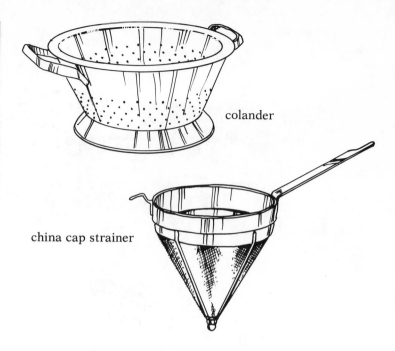
colander

china cap strainer

mallet—a hammer

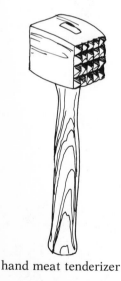

hand meat tenderizer

A **hand meat tenderizer** is a **mallet** with a cast aluminium head used to break the muscle fibres of tough cuts of meat, making them more tender.

A **parisienne scoop** is a small, stainless steel cup which is shaped like a half ball and attached to a handle. It is used to cut and shape fruit and some vegetables into small balls. Another name for it is a **melon ball scoop**.

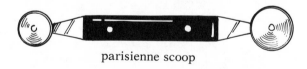

parisienne scoop

Baking Tools

A **dough cutter** is a wide, rectangular metal blade with a wooden handle. It is used for cutting, dividing and lifting dough. It is also used for scraping dough boards.

A **plastic scraper** is a thin, flexible piece of plastic which is used to scrape bowls when mixing cake batters so that all ingredients are included in the mixture.

A **palette knife** has a wide, flexible blade with a rounded tip. It is used mainly for spreading icings on cakes.

A **pastry wheel** is a stainless steel disc with sharp edges mounted on a handle. It is used to cut all kinds of pastry.

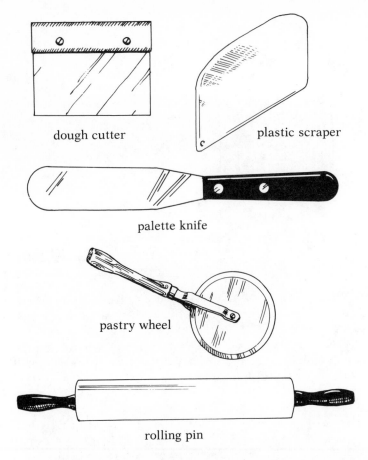

dough cutter

plastic scraper

palette knife

pastry wheel

rolling pin

A **rolling pin** is a long roller made of wood with handles at each end. It is used for rolling out all kinds of dough to the desired thickness.

A **pie and cake marker** is a circular, metal frame which is placed over cakes and pies to cut accurate portions. It has wire guides for the cutting of various portion sizes.

A **flour sifter** is a round, metal container with a screen or mesh attached at the bottom. It is used to sift flour and blend dry ingredients to produce a light and **uniform** finished product.

A **pastry bag** is a cone-shaped bag made of water repellent material such as plastic. It is used with pastry tubes to decorate cakes, cookies and **canapés**.

A **pastry tube** is a small, cone-shaped, metal tube which fits into the narrow end of a pastry bag for decorating. These tubes are available in a variety of decorating tips.

A **pastry brush**, much like a paint brush, is made of bristles attached to a handle. It is used mainly to apply egg wash to certain types of pastry. It may also be used to spread thin icings.

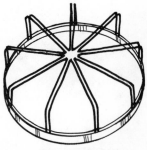

pie and cake marker

uniform—always the same

canapés—small, savoury appetizers made on toast

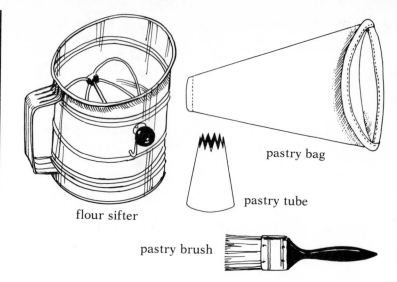

flour sifter

pastry bag

pastry tube

pastry brush

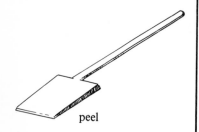

peel

A **peel** is a long-handled, flat piece of wood shaped like a paddle. It is used to place items in the rear of large bake ovens.

A **bench brush** is a long wooden- or plastic-handled brush which is used to brush excess flour from the bench when working with doughs.

bench brush

POTS, PANS AND CONTAINERS

For Mixing

Bowls are usually made of stainless steel and are available in many sizes. They are used for mixing and combining ingredients in preparation for cooking.

For Cooking

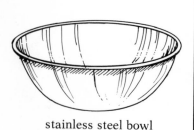

stainless steel bowl

gauge—a measure of thickness

faucet—a tap

A **stock pot** is a large, straight-sided pot with loop handles for easy lifting. It may be made of heavy **gauge** aluminium or stainless steel. The stock pot is used for boiling and simmering food when making stock. It may be equipped with a **faucet** for drawing off the liquid contents.

A **sauce pot** is a large, deep pot with loop handles for easy lifting. It is used for cooking on top of the stove when stirring or whipping the contents is necessary.

A **sauce pan** is a smaller version of the sauce pot. It has one long handle and is used for cooking smaller amounts of food.

A **sautoir** is a large, shallow, straight-sided pan with a long handle and a loop handle opposite. It is made of heavy gauge metal and is used for sautéing or shallow frying larger amounts of food at high temperatures.

A **sauté pan** is a small shallow pan with sloping sides and a long handle. It is used for sautéing or shallow frying small amounts of food.

A **cast iron skillet** is a heavy, shallow pan which retains heat well. It is used for frying and pan broiling.

A **brazier** is a large, shallow-walled pot with a large surface area for good contact with the heat. It has loop handles and is used for searing, stewing and braising meats.

A **double boiler** consists of two containers. The bottom container holds boiling water. The second container fits into the bottom container and is suspended in the boiling water. It is used to cook foods such as puddings and

stock pot

sauce pot

sauce pan

sauté pan

sautoir

cast iron skillet

brazier

double boiler

scorch—burn slightly

bake pan

cream fillings which would **scorch** if cooked over direct heat.

A **bake pan** is a large, shallow, rectangular pan with loop handles. It is used for baking.

A **roasting pan** is a large, rectangular pan with medium-high sides. It is used for roasting meats.

A **sheet pan** is shallow and rectangular. It is used for baking sweet goods.

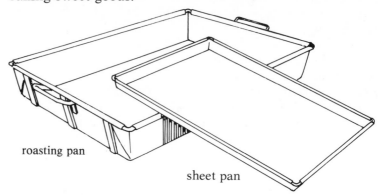

roasting pan

sheet pan

For Storage

A **canister** is a small storage container with a close fitting lid. It is for storing items such as herbs and spices that are used in small amounts.

A **bin** is a large, rectangular storage container with a close-fitting lid. It is used for storing **staples** such as flour, sugar and rice. Since these bins are large and heavy when they are full, they are usually mounted on **casters** for ease of movement.

staples—most important
products or most
common products
casters—small wheels

canisters

bin

LARGE EQUIPMENT

Equipment refers to the more complicated tools in the kitchen. This includes large, stationary equipment such as ranges, mixers and ovens, as well as smaller power equipment like toasters, slicers and choppers. Since each kitchen is different and there is a wide variety of equipment available, we will only deal with the basic equipment you will encounter. Your instructor will, no doubt, demonstrate and explain the equipment contained in the kitchen where you will be working.

A **deep fat fryer** is a large, deep frying kettle which is thermostatically controlled. It will hold 10 to 20 kg (20 to 45 lb.) of shortening, depending on the size of the fryer.

The **steamer unit** is available in various sizes. It cooks food with pressurized steam. Steam cooking units are generally used in large institutional kitchens such as are found in hospitals and **commissaries**.

The **mixing machine** is one of the most versatile pieces of kitchen equipment. It can perform many other functions besides mixing because of the various attachments

commissaries—large kitchens that serve several outlets

deep fat fryer

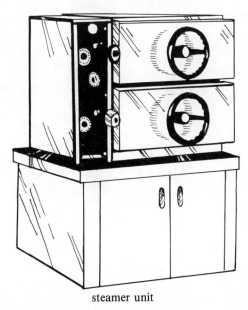

steamer unit

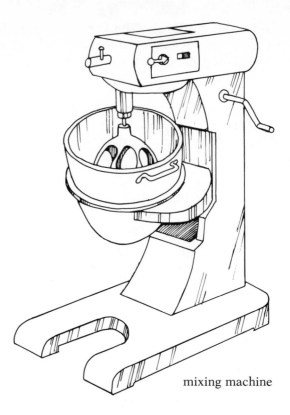

mixing machine

that are available for it. These attachments enable the machine to grind, chop, slice and shred foods.

The **slicing machine** is primarily used for slicing cooked meats. However, it can also be used to shred such foods as lettuce and cabbage. It has a regulator which controls the thickness of the slices you cut. Because of the sharp, high-speed, revolving blade, slicing machines are provided with many safety features to protect the user.

A **food chopper** has both a revolving bowl and blade to chop foods. Like the mixing machine, it has attachments for grinding, shredding and slicing food.

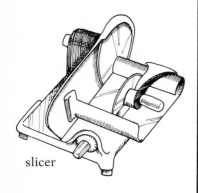

slicer

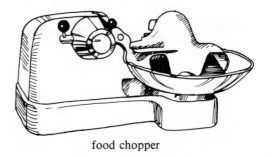

food chopper

The **convection oven** is like a **conventional** oven except that there is a fan inside it which circulates the air. The circulating distributes heat evenly to all parts of the oven so that it cooks more uniformly. This reduces shrinkage and cooking time. The convection oven is also more energy efficient than the conventional oven.

conventional—customary or ordinary

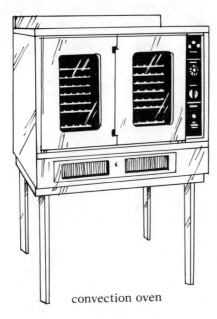

convection oven

Find the Answers to These Questions

1. Name the tools which are used to perform the following tasks:
   (a) chopping through bones
   (b) sectioning citrus fruits
   (c) serving liquids
   (d) dicing food
   (e) straining soups and sauces
2. What is a countermass?
3. Describe the difference between tools and equipment.
4. What is the function of a double boiler?
5. How does a convection oven differ from a conventional oven?

CHAPTER 5
NUTRITION

Watch for These Words

elements
regulate
converts
digested
beneficial
component
immobilize
fulfill

oxidation
essential
tissues
enzymes
hormones
concentrated
puberty
clotting

enriched
elimination
lubricant
soluble
absorbed
proportionate
derive
alkaline

How to Use These Words

1. Before the doctor could move the injured man, he had to __XXXX__ the fracture so that it would not be jarred.
2. __XXXX__ of waste products from body cells is an important function of water.
3. At __XXXX__, calcium is extremely important in the growth of bones and teeth.
4. Proteins build and repair body __XXXX__.
5. Vitamins A, D, E and K are __XXXX__ into the body when we eat food fats.
6. When food is __XXXX__ in the body, the nutrients are released for the body's use.
7. Vitamins that dissolve during the cooking of vegetables in water are called water-__XXXX__ vitamins.
8. Carbohydrates are one of the __XXXX__ of good nutrition.
9. Vitamin K ensures normal __XXXX__ of the blood.
10. Nutrients __XXXX__ body processes.
11. You can __XXXX__ the benefit of water-soluble vitamins if the cooking water is used in soup.
12. "Empty calories" provide no __XXXX__ nutrients to the body.

13. Bread and cereals are often ___XXXX___ by the addition of vitamins.
14. ___XXXX___ are substances secreted by glands in the body.
15. The process that ___XXXX___ food into energy is called metabolism.
16. Fats are aided in their ___XXXX___ by carbohydrates.
17. Carbohydrates, fats, minerals and vitamins are all ___XXXX___ of nutrition.
18. Water acts as a ___XXXX___ in the passage and digestion of food.
19. Carbohydrates ___XXXX___ most of the body's energy needs.
20. ___XXXX___ speed up the process of metabolism.
21. Because baking soda is ___XXXX___, it destroys water-soluble vitamins.
22. Fats provide a ___XXXX___ form of energy.
23. Proper eating habits are ___XXXX___ for good nutrition.
24. Water-soluble vitamins are lost in amounts ___XXXX___ to the length of soaking time.

elements—parts of

regulate—adjust

converts—changes

In today's health conscious world, it is not enough for the professional cook to master the art of food preparation. He or she must also take responsibility for preparing meals that are nutritionally sound and balanced. This is not as difficult as it may appear. With the vast array of foods available to us, it is possible to prepare a wide variety of dishes which provide the proper nutritional **elements** necessary for good health. Today a good understanding of basic nutrition is essential for the professional cook.

Nutrition is the science that studies the food you eat and the way your body uses it. All food is composed of elements known as nutrients. Nutrients are the chemical compounds found in food which help your body grow, repair and maintain itself and which produce energy and **regulate** body processes. Examples of nutrients found in food are proteins, carbohydrates, fats, vitamins, and minerals. The nutrients in food are vital because they nourish every part of your body. Only through eating food can you obtain these nutrients.

The body **converts** food into energy by a process known as metabolism. Metabolism is a continuous process which goes on constantly, even when you are asleep. It starts in the digestive system, where the food is broken down into its simplest parts. Then the blood transports these parts to the body's cells, where they are changed into energy.

A calorie is the unit used to measure the amount of heat energy produced by the body. One calorie measures the amount of heat required to raise the temperature of one kilogram of water by one degree Celsius (1°C). The kilojoule is the metric measurement which replaces the calorie. In one calorie there are 4.2 kilojoules. Calories and kilojoules are also ways of stating the amount of heat energy that can be expected from any one food. For example, if 225 mL of a soft drink contain 420 kJ, this means that when the soft drink is **digested** in the body, it will release that amount of heat energy for the body's use.

All foods contain kilojoules. Some have more than others. When more kilojoules are consumed than the body can use, the extra kilojoules are stored in the body as fat. If fewer kilojoules are eaten than the body can use, the body's mass will decrease as kilojoules stored in the form of fat are used up. The amount of kilojoules that the body needs depends on age, sex, height, body build and the amount of physical activity that the body engages in. We often hear the phrase "empty calories" during conversations about nutrition. This means that the food eaten provides us with calories (kilojoules) but nothing else. None of the beneficial nutrients required by the body are provided by these foods. Examples of foods in this category are soft drinks, potato chips and candy.

So far we have dealt with food as a source of heat energy for the body. However, food is also vital if the body is to grow, repair and maintain itself and to regulate the body processes. The human body starts out as a tiny egg and develops and grows to a full-size adult. The **component** parts of the body, such as the bones, muscles and blood, must be built from the food which we eat.

If you have ever broken a bone, a doctor can **immobilize** and set it. However, the healing process comes about through the body's ability to repair itself. This process depends on the food you eat.

The body keeps itself functioning properly using the food which is eaten. Body cells which are worn out must be replaced. Digestive juices are constantly being used up and must be replaced. This kind of maintenance depends on the food which is eaten. The body also regulates its processes. If extra energy is required to perform a task, the body will automatically produce this extra energy if the right kinds and amounts of food have been consumed.

digested—converted for absorption

"empty calories"

component—the parts that make up the whole
immobilize—restrict the movement of

NUTRIENTS

Carbohydrates

Carbohydrates provide the body with its main source of energy. They are found in large quantities in inexpensive foods. Every body process uses up energy, and it is important that these energy requirements are always met. If the body does not get enough energy from carbohydrates, it will start using up some fats and proteins to **fulfill** its energy needs. Carbohydrates help in **oxidation** of fats in the body so that the energy of the fats can be released. Grain or cereals made from grains are a main source of carbohydrates. Grains such as wheat, corn, oats and rice are common sources of carbohydrates in North America. As well as cereals, products made from flour, such as bread, cakes, pastries and pasta are sources of carbohydrates. Root vegetables are another source of carbohydrates. Since the root of a plant is the storehouse of energy for the rest of the plant, such vegetables as potatoes, turnips, carrots and beets are good sources of carbohydrates. In addition, seed vegetables such as dried peas and beans are another good source because of their sugar content. Firm fruits, such as bananas, and dried fruits are higher in carbohydrates than more watery fruits like melons or strawberries.

Proteins

Proteins are essential to the survival of all living things. They build and repair the body **tissues**. Proteins form essential substances such as **enzymes** and **hormones**, which are the regulators of body functions. When the needs for growth and repair of the body tissues have been met, the remaining proteins are broken down and stored in the form of fat, which becomes a source of energy. Protein comes from animal sources and from plant sources. Animal sources include meat, fish, poultry, eggs, milk and cheese. Plant sources include grains, dried peas and beans, nuts, cereals and breads.

Fats

Fats serve as a **concentrated** form of energy. They provide about 2¼ times as much energy as equivalent amounts of carbohydrates or proteins. There are two kinds of fats: animal fat and vegetable fat. Sources of fats include meat, fish, eggs, cream, nuts and fried foods. Fats protect the body from sudden changes in outside temperatures and help to maintain a constant internal body temperature. In

fulfill—satisfy
oxidation—the process of combining with oxygen

tissues—masses of cells which perform particular functions in the body
enzymes—speed up metabolism
hormones—substances secreted by glands

concentrated—increased in strength

addition, stored fats deposited around vital organs protect these organs from sudden shocks. Fats take a longer time to digest and therefore help to delay the onset of hunger.

Minerals

Minerals are present in the body for growth and maintenance. There are more than fifteen different minerals in the body. Of these, the most important ones are calcium, phosphorus, iron and iodine.

The body contains more **calcium** than any other mineral. At **puberty**, calcium is extremely important because it makes your teeth and bones grow and strengthen. Calcium also regulates such body processes as **clotting** of the blood, the pumping action of the heart and the improvement of muscle tone. The most important source of calcium is milk and milk products such as cheese, ice cream and yogurt. Smaller amounts of calcium are contained in green leafy vegetables like cabbage and broccoli.

puberty—the age at which one can reproduce

clotting—becoming thick and forming a solid mass, or clot

A source of calcium (Courtesy of the Ontario Ministry of Agriculture and Food)

Most of the **iron** in your body is found in the blood, helping the red blood cells carry oxygen to the different parts of the body. Liver is the richest source of iron. Meat and poultry are good sources, as are green leafy vegetables and egg yolks. Whole grain and **enriched** cereals, flours, breads and pasta are less expensive sources of iron.

Phosphorus is as important as calcium in the formation of strong teeth and bones. It also helps the body to absorb

enriched—supplied with extra vitamins and minerals

other nutrients. Sources of phosphorus are meat, fish, poultry, eggs, milk, cheese and nuts.

Iodine is found in the body in very small amounts. However, it is important for the proper functioning of the thyroid gland, which regulates the metabolism in your body. Iodine is added to table salt to ensure that most people get an adequate supply. Seafood is a good natural source of iodine.

Water

Water is a very important nutrient. We can only survive for a few days without it. Water is the transporter of fats, sugars, amino acids and minerals in the body. It carries these nutrients to the individual body cells. Just as water is important as the transporter of nutrients, it is also important in carrying waste products from the body cells to the kidneys, skin and lungs for **elimination**. Water also acts as a **lubricant** in the passage and digestion of food and as a regulator for body temperature. While water is available from the tap, it is also present in milk, soups, juices and even solid foods.

elimination—removal
lubricant—coating which makes parts move more smoothly

Vitamins

Vitamins are chemical substances needed by the body in small amounts for growth and good health. They make it possible for the foods we eat to perform their necessary functions. Vitamins regulate the body processes and prevent specific diseases. All vitamins are **soluble** in either fat or water. The fat-soluble vitamins (A, D, E and K) dissolve in fat and are less easily destroyed in the preparation of food than water-soluble vitamins. The water-soluble vitamins (B and C) dissolve in water and are easily lost in food preparation.

soluble—can be dissolved

Fat-soluble vitamins are **absorbed** into the body with the food fats that we consume. They cannot dissolve in cooking water or be destroyed by heat. When more of the fat-soluble vitamins are consumed than are necessary for daily needs, most of the excess is stored in the liver for later use when our intake is not enough for daily needs.

absorbed—taken in

Vitamin A helps keep our skin healthy and attractive. It also helps build and strengthen bones and teeth and improve our night vision. Good natural sources of vitamin A are egg yolks, liver, butter, cheese, dark green and yellow vegetables and deep yellow fruits.

Vitamin D makes it possible for the body to use calcium to build strong bones and teeth. Sources of vitamin D are

enriched milk and margarine, fish liver oils and sunshine. Human skin has the ability to absorb ultraviolet rays from the sunlight and convert them to vitamin D.

Vitamin E helps to protect the body's supplies of vitamins A and C. It also aids in the formation of blood cells. Good sources of this vitamin are vegetable oils, wheat germ, margarine, whole grains, eggs, liver, fruits and vegetables.

Vitamin K ensures the normal clotting of the blood. Good sources of this vitamin are green and yellow vegetables.

Water-soluble vitamins are vitamins that dissolve in water and are easily lost through careless food preparation. If fruits or vegetables are allowed to soak in water for any length of time, loss of vitamins B and C occurs in amounts **proportionate** to the length of soaking time. To minimize this vitamin loss in fruits and vegetables, wash them in cold water rather than soaking them.

proportionate—in proportion to

Additional loss of vitamins B and C occurs during the cooking of vegetables. Vegetables that contain vitamins B and C should be cooked in large pieces in as little water as possible, with care being taken not to overcook the vegetables. In addition, the cooking water should be used in soups or sauces to **derive** the benefit of the dissolved vitamins.

derive—receive

Vitamin loss in meat can occur when frozen meat is thawed. The juice which drips from the meat as it is defrosting contains water-soluble vitamins. This juice should be collected in a pan and used in a gravy to go with the meat dish. The use of baking soda to preserve the colour in green vegetables also contributes to vitamin loss. Since baking soda is **alkaline**, it will destroy the water-soluble vitamins.

alkaline—capable of neutralizing acids; the opposite of acidic

Vitamin C can be destroyed when exposed to air. The added exposure to sunlight will speed the process. Foods which contain vitamin C should be properly stored in covered containers in a cool, dark place. They should be cooked and served as soon as possible.

Thiamine (vitamin B₁) promotes good appetite and aids in digestion. It helps keep the nervous system healthy and releases the energy from carbohydrates. Good sources of thiamine are pork, whole grain breads and cereals, enriched breads and cereals, pasta and dried peas, beans and lentils.

Riboflavin (vitamin B₂) contributes to healthy skin, eyes and mouth. It also helps the body's cells use oxygen. Good sources of riboflavin are milk, cheese, eggs, salmon, leafy green vegetables and organ meats such as liver.

Niacin helps to promote normal growth and development. It also aids in the healthy functioning of the intestines and the nervous system. Good sources of niacin are meat, fish, poultry, enriched breads and cereals, milk, cheese, eggs, nuts and dried peas and beans.

The B vitamins can be stored in the body to provide for the body's needs for a full week of normal activity.

Vitamin C promotes the healthy formation and repair of bones, teeth and gums. It promotes the healing of wounds and helps the body to resist infection. Vitamin C also helps to maintain healthy blood vessels and reduces bruising. Good sources of vitamin C are all citrus fruits and their juices, strawberries, cantaloupe, tomatoes, broccoli, cauliflower, Brussels sprouts, green cabbage and turnips. Vitamin C cannot be stored in the body. Thus, a daily supply of this vitamin is necessary to keep the body functioning normally.

CANADA'S FOOD GUIDE

Health and Welfare Canada recommends that you eat a variety of foods from each of four groups every day for good nutrition.

Milk and Milk Products

Recommended amounts per day are:
Children up to eleven years	2–3 servings
Adolescents	3–4 servings
Pregnant and nursing women	3–4 servings
Adults	2 servings

Skim, 2%, whole, buttermilk, reconstituted dry or evaporated milk may be used as a beverage or as the main ingredient in other foods. Cheese may also be chosen.
Examples of one serving are:
250 mL (1 cup) milk, yogurt or cottage cheese
45 g (1 1/2 oz.) cheddar or processed cheese

Meat and Alternates

Two servings per day are recommended for adults.
Examples of one serving are:
60–90 g (2–3 oz.) cooked lean meat, poultry, liver or fish
60 mL (2 oz.) peanut butter
250 mL (1 cup) cooked dried peas, beans or lentils
80–250 mL (1/3–1 cup) nuts or seeds
60 g (2 oz.) cheddar, processed or cottage cheese
2 eggs

Bread and Cereals

Three to five servings per day of whole grain or enriched grain products are recommended. (Whole grain products are preferred.)
Examples of one serving are:
1 slice of bread
125–250 mL (½–1 cup) cooked or ready-to-eat cereal
1 roll or muffin
125–250 mL (½–1 cup) cooked rice, macaroni or spaghetti.

Fruits and Vegetables

Four to five servings per day are recommended. Include at least two vegetables. Choose a variety of both vegetables and fruits. Eat them cooked or raw or drink their juices. Include yellow or green or green leafy vegetables.
Examples of one serving are:
125 mL (½ cup) vegetables or fruits
125 mL (½ cup) juice
1 medium potato, carrot, tomato, peach, apple, orange or banana

In addition, a supplement of vitamin D is recommended if your milk does not contain added vitamin D.

(Courtesy of the Ontario Ministry of Industry and Tourism)

Find the Answers to These Questions

1. What is the meaning of nutrition?
2. Explain the process known as metabolism.

3. What are kilojoules?
4. What are the functions of carbohydrates?
5. When the body takes in too much protein, what happens to the extra protein?
6. There are two kinds of fat. What are they?
7. Why is calcium so important to your body?
8. What is the main source of iodine?
9. One nutrient is known as a "transporter." Which one is it?
10. Name the water-soluble vitamins.
11. Why is it important to be careful in the preparation of food containing water-soluble vitamins?
12. Why do we need a daily intake of vitamin C?

CHAPTER 6
APPETIZERS

Watch for These Words

whet	precede	thoroughly
unique	infinite	variation
stimulating	savoury	incorporated
dainty	appropriate	consistency
tart	supplement	blemishes
cloying	jumbo	
stemware	surrounded	

How to Use These Words

1. The icing on the cake was so sweet that it had a __XXXX__ taste.
2. Shrimp are available in many sizes from tiny to __XXXX__.
3. When the ingredients were all ready, they were __XXXX__ into a mixture.
4. The assortment of canapés was __XXXX__ and attractive.
5. The instructions in the recipe stated that the ingredients must be __XXXX__ blended.
6. The mixture was blended to a very smooth __XXXX__.
7. The creative imagination of the cook helped him to produce some __XXXX__ appetizers.
8. The cook produced an __XXXX__ variety of appetizers.
9. The cook rejected the radishes for the relish tray because they had many __XXXX__.
10. Appetizers are designed to __XXXX__ or stimulate the appetite.
11. __XXXX__ garnishes add to the eye appeal of appetizers.
12. The recipe did not allow for any __XXXX__ in ingredients.
13. Appetizers are meant to __XXXX__ the main meal.

14. The hors-d'oeuvres were very ___XXXX___ to the appetite.
15. As the host stood in the centre of the room, the guests ___XXXX___ him to enquire about the food.
16. The fruit cocktail had a ___XXXX___ and tangy taste.
17. The hot hors-d'oeuvres were very ___XXXX___.
18. The cook used canned fruit to ___XXXX___ the fresh fruit in the cocktail.
19. The shrimp cocktail was served in elegant ___XXXX___.

whet—sharpen or excite

unique—unusual

Appetizers are small portions of food which are served to **whet** or stimulate the appetite for the meal to come. Appetizers should not satisfy the appetite by themselves. Appetizers may be served in many different ways and may be liquid or solid. They present **unique** opportunities for the cook to demonstrate his or her imagination and creativity.

stimulating—exciting
dainty—delicate

Appetizers must have eye appeal as well as taste appeal. They should have colourful ingredients for eye appeal and **stimulating** ingredients for taste appeal. They must be **dainty** and bite sized. There is a wide variety of appetizers, but they generally fall into the following categories:
cocktails
appetizer salads
hors-d'oeuvres
canapés
relishes

COCKTAILS

tart—sour
cloying—excessively sweet and dulling to the taste

Cocktails may be made from vegetable juices, fruit juices, fruit, seafood and shellfish. Juices should be well chilled and **tart** or tangy in taste rather than sweet or **cloying**. This will stimulate the appetite rather than dull it. Fruit, seafood and shellfish appetizers should be well chilled, fresh and attractive in appearance. They should also be cut in bite-sized pieces and presented in appropriate **stemware** or serving dishes.

stemware—glassware with a supporting stem

APPETIZER SALADS

Appetizer salads usually include pickled herring, smoked salmon, smoked oysters, chopped chicken livers, stuffed eggs, asparagus tips, artichoke hearts and various pâtés.

Appetizer salads should be served on a base of fresh lettuce leaves that are crisp and clean. They should be well chilled and tastefully garnished for eye appeal.

HORS-D'OEUVRES

These are small portions of well-seasoned foods served either hot or cold. Traditionally they should **precede** the main meal. However, hors-d'oeuvres are often served at cocktail parties or as late evening snacks. They should be small enough to be eaten with the fingers or a toothpick. If they are served at the table, hors-d'oeuvres are usually eaten with a small fork.

precede—come before

There is an **infinite** variety of hors-d'oeuvres which may be made from any combination of **savoury** foods. Examples of hors-d'oeuvres include sausage rolls, stuffed mushrooms, stuffed eggs, miniature pizzas or quiches, oysters wrapped in bacon, stuffed celery, rolled or stuffed meats, bite-sized pieces of cheese or meat, meatballs, filled bouchées and spiced fruits and vegetables. Always remember to serve hot hors-d'oeuvres piping hot and cold hors-d'oeuvres well chilled.

infinite—limitless
savoury—tasty

CANAPÉS

Canapés are appetizers which are like small open-face sandwiches. They are made from combinations of flavoured butters, savoury spreads and bite-sized pieces of food. Canapés are always served on a base of bread, toast or crackers and are usually served cold. Again, an infinite variety of canapés can be prepared from many combinations of food. These are limited only by the imagination and creativity of the cook.

Canapés are an excellent way of using up leftovers, which can be made into many tasty spreads. Some examples of ingredients used in the production of canapés are smoked salmon, sardines, smoked oysters, anchovies, caviar, meats, cheeses, and meat, fish and dairy pastes or spreads. When preparing canapés, imagination and variety are important. Different varieties of bread should be used. Many shapes can be cut from toast or bread. Some crackers can be used, but the variety of shapes available in crackers is limited. The bread, toast or crackers are spread with flavoured butters. Savoury pastes may be piped onto these using a pastry bag and an **appropriate** decorating tube. Bite-sized pieces of other foods may also be used.

appropriate—suitable

aspic—savoury jelly of meat or vegetable juices

Finally, a colourful and appropriate garnish is added. If canapés are to be refrigerated for later use, a light glaze of clear **aspic** may be applied. For quantity production of canapés, slice loaves of bread lengthwise, apply the various ingredients, and then cut in a variety of shapes.

RELISHES

Relishes are usually brought to the table in dishes sprinkled with crushed ice to keep the ingredients well chilled and crisp. Relishes normally include the following: radishes, celery hearts, green onions, carrots, stuffed olives, ripe olives, pickles and other raw vegetables. The vegetables used may be cut in a variety of shapes such as roses, curls and sticks.

(Courtesy of the Ontario Ministry of Agriculture and Food)

RECIPES

Cocktails

Fruit cocktail may be made with fresh or canned fruit or a combination of both. In season, use the fresh varieties available and **supplement** them with canned vegetables if necessary.

supplement—add to

Fruit Cocktail

Yield: 4 portions

12 fresh strawberries
 8 apple wedges, unpeeled
 4 slices of pineapple
 4 peach halves
 4 pear halves
12 grapes
 8 red maraschino cherries
 4 mint leaves
   lettuce

Method

1. **Dice** the fruit in bite-sized pieces.
2. Gently mix the diced fruit in a mixing bowl.
3. Place a base of lettuce leaves in each of four 90 mL (3 oz.) cocktail glasses.
4. Divide the fruit cocktail mixture into the four glasses.
5. Garnish each portion with two maraschino cherries and one mint leaf.

dice—cut into small cubes

Melon Cocktail

Yield: 4 portions

16 watermelon balls
16 honeydew melon balls
16 cantaloupe balls
 4 mint leaves
   lettuce

Method

1. Using a parisienne scoop, cut the melon balls.
2. Place a base of lettuce in each of four 90 mL (3 oz.) cocktail glasses.
3. Arrange the melon balls attractively in the glasses. Garnish each with one mint leaf.

Shrimp Cocktail

Yield: 1 portion

A great variety of shrimp is available on the market to-day. They range in size from tiny Alaskan shrimp to **jumbo** shrimp from the Gulf of Mexico. All sizes may be used successfully in shrimp cocktails.

jumbo—very large

6 medium shrimp, cooked
30 mL (1 oz.) cocktail sauce (See Chapter 8.)
    shredded lettuce
    lemon wedge

Method

1. Place shredded lettuce in a 90 mL (3 oz.) cocktail glass.
2. Arrange the shrimp on top of the shredded lettuce.
3. Top with cocktail sauce and garnish with a lemon wedge.
    Any shellfish cocktail may be prepared in the same manner. Crabmeat, lobster or mixed seafood may be substituted for the shrimp.

Appetizer Salads

Avocado Stuffed with Crabmeat   Yield: 2 portions

1		ripe avocado
120 g	(4 oz.)	crabmeat, frozen or canned
15 g	(1 tbsp.)	green pepper, finely diced
15 g	(1 tbsp.)	pimiento, finely diced
30 mL	(1 oz.)	cocktail sauce (See Chapter 8.)
30 mL	(1 oz.)	mayonnaise
5 mL	(1 tsp.)	lemon juice
2		lemon wedges
		parsley

Method

1. Drain the crabmeat by gently squeezing out the excess moisture.
2. Place the crabmeat in a mixing bowl.
3. Combine the cocktail sauce, mayonnaise, lemon juice and finely diced peppers and pimiento in a bowl and mix well.
4. Add the sauce mixture to the crabmeat and mix.
5. Cut the avocado in half lengthwise.
6. Carefully remove the centre stone without damaging the fruit.
7. Cut a thin slice from the bottom of each half so that the avocado will sit firmly on the plate.
8. Place the crabmeat mixture in the avocado halves.
9. Garnish with a lemon wedge and parsley.

Eggs à la Russe
Yield: 4 portions

russe—Russian

2		eggs, hard boiled
120 mL	(4 oz.)	Russian dressing (See page 191.)
		lettuce
		parsley

Method

1. Place a base of shredded lettuce on a 10 cm plate.
2. Cut the hard-boiled eggs in half lengthwise.
3. Place one-half of an egg on the shredded lettuce.
4. Cover the half of the egg with 30 mL (1 oz.) of Russian dressing.
5. Garnish with parsley.

Beef Salad
Approximate yield: 4 portions

120 g	(4 oz.)	leftover beef, thinly sliced
120 mL	(4 oz.)	oil and vinegar dressing
30 g	(1 oz.)	onion, finely diced
15 mL	(1 tbsp.)	parsley, chopped
		lettuce
		hard-boiled egg, sliced

Method

1. Marinate the beef in oil and vinegar dressing, to which the diced onion and chopped parsley have been added.
2. Marinate for 2 h.
3. Place a lettuce leaf on a 10 cm plate.
4. Place 30 g (1 oz.) marinated beef attractively on the lettuce.
5. Garnish with sliced hard-boiled egg.

Mushroom Salad
Approximate yield: 6 portions

450 g	(1 lb.)	raw mushrooms, sliced
45 mL	(3 tbsp.)	salad oil
15 mL	(1 tbsp.)	lemon juice
1 mL	(1/4 tsp.)	sugar
		lettuce
3		tomatoes, sliced
		dill pickle, sliced
		pickled onions
		salt to taste
		cayenne to taste

Method

1. Marinate the sliced mushrooms in the dressing made with the oil, lemon juice, sugar, salt and cayenne for 1 h.
2. Place a lettuce leaf on a 10 cm plate.
3. Divide the marinated mushrooms and place on the lettuce leaves.
4. **Surround** the mushrooms with sliced tomatoes.
5. Garnish with sliced dill pickle and a pickled onion.

surround—encircle

Antipasto
Approximate yield: 10 portions

250 mL	(1 cup)	eggplant, peeled and diced
65 mL	(¼ cup)	onion, diced
65 mL	(¼ cup)	mushrooms, diced
1		clove of garlic, minced
65 mL	(¼ cup)	salad oil
125 mL	(½ cup)	tomato paste
65 mL	(¼ cup)	water
65 mL	(¼ cup)	wine vinegar
65 mL	(¼ cup)	green peppers, diced
125 mL	(½ cup)	cauliflower
30 g	(1 oz.)	stuffed olives, sliced
30 g	(1 oz.)	ripe olives, pitted and sliced
5 mL	(1 tsp.)	sugar
2 mL	(½ tsp.)	oregano
65 mL	(¼ cup)	celery, diced and precooked

Method

1. Place the eggplant, onions, mushrooms, garlic, oil, green peppers, cauliflower and precooked celery in a braising pot.
2. Cover and cook gently for about 10 min with gentle stirring.
3. Add the remaining ingredients.
4. Continue cooking until all the ingredients are tender.
5. Remove from the heat and allow to cool.
6. Refrigerate overnight to allow the flavours to blend.
7. Place a lettuce leaf on a 10 cm plate.
8. Put a small portion of the cooked mixture on the lettuce.
9. Add small portions of any or all of the following: sliced Italian salami, sliced Italian capicola, tuna fish and sardines.
10. Garnish with parsley.

Hors-d'oeuvres

Meatballs

Approximate yield: 36 meatballs

450 g	(1 lb.)	ground chuck roast
30 mL	(2 tbsp.)	onions, diced
250 mL	(1 cup)	breadcrumbs, moistened with milk
2 mL	(½ tsp.)	thyme
15 mL	(1 tbsp.)	oil
		salt and pepper to taste
1		clove of garlic, minced

Method

1. Sauté the onions and the garlic in the oil.
2. Combine all the ingredients thoroughly, including the onions and garlic.
3. Form the mixture into small meatballs and place on a greased sheet pan.
4. Bake in a 180°C (350°F) oven until done.
5. Serve with a sauce such as barbecue sauce, curry sauce or caper sauce in a chafing dish. (See Chapter 8 for sauce recipes.)

Mushrooms à la Grecque

Approximate yield: 8 portions

grecque—Greek

Vegetables à la grecque are usually served cold as an hors-d'oeuvre, with some of the cooking liquid used as a sauce. The method of cooking these vegetables always includes the use of water or stock with olive oil, lemon juice and various herbs and spices.

675 g	(1½ lb.)	mushrooms
250 mL	(1 cup)	boiling water
60 mL	(2 oz.)	white wine vinegar
60 mL	(2 oz.)	olive oil
45 mL	(3 tbsp.)	lemon juice
1		bay leaf
6		whole peppercorns
2		sprigs of parsley
		salt to taste

Method

1. Wash the mushrooms and save the stems for soup or sauces.
2. Cut the mushroom caps into quarters if they are large.

3. Place all ingredients, except mushrooms, in a sauce pan.
4. Cover and cook slowly for 5 min.
5. Add the mushrooms and cook for 8 to 10 min over low heat.
6. Let stand and cool in the cooking liquid.

Other vegetables may be cooked by this method with some **variation** in cooking times, depending on the type of vegetables used.

variation—change

Chicken and Mushroom Tartlets   Yield: 12 tartlets

		unsweetened pastry dough (See Chapter 15.)
375 mL	(1½ cup)	cooked chicken, finely diced
250 mL	(1 cup)	raw mushrooms, finely diced
185 mL	(¾ cup)	béchamel sauce (See Chapter 8.)
30 mL	(2 tbsp.)	butter
3		egg yolks, beaten
		salt, pepper and lemon juice to taste

Method

1. Line small tartlet moulds with thinly rolled pastry dough and set aside.
2. Combine chicken, mushrooms, béchamel sauce, butter and seasonings.
3. Cook over medium heat for 3 to 4 min, then remove from the heat.
4. Add a little of the hot mixture to the beaten egg yolks, and then add this to the rest of the hot mixture.
5. Mix thoroughly.
6. Spoon the mixture into the tartlet shells.
7. Place the filled shells on a baking sheet and bake at 220°C (425°F) for 10 to 12 min, or until the pastry has browned.
8. Serve as a hot hors-d'oeuvre.

Stuffed Mushroom Caps   Yield: 24 mushroom caps

24		raw mushroom caps, large
500 mL	(2 cups)	cooked shrimp, diced
500 mL	(2 cups)	cooked rice
20 mL	(4 tsp.)	parsley, chopped
5 mL	(1 tsp.)	salt
1 mL	(¼ tsp.)	thyme
125 mL	(½ cup)	cheddar cheese, grated

Method

1. Wash the mushroom caps. Let drain and dry.
2. Combine the remaining ingredients, except the cheese.
3. Mix together in a mixing bowl.
4. Spoon the mixture generously into the mushroom caps.
5. Sprinkle with grated cheddar cheese.
6. Bake in the oven at 190°C (375°F) for 10 min.
7. Serve as a hot hors-d'oeuvre.

Canapés

Flavoured Butters

These flavoured butters may be spread or piped onto canapés as decoration. The butter to be used should be at room temperature to make it easier to work with. All ingredients to be **incorporated** into the softened butter should be finely chopped or puréed. This will ensure that pastry tubes do not become clogged when the flavoured butters are being piped onto canapés.

incorporated—combined with

Anchovy Butter   Add 60 mL (2 oz.) of puréed anchovy fillets to 450 g (1 lb.) of butter. Blend this mixture to a smooth **consistency**.

Chive Butter   Add a small bunch of finely chopped chives to 450 g (1 lb.) of butter. Blend well to a smooth consistency.

consistency—degree of density

Garlic Butter   Add 1 clove of puréed garlic to 450 g (1 lb.) of butter. Blend this mixture well to a smooth consistency.

Horseradish Butter   Add 120 mL (4 oz.) of creamed horseradish to 450 g (1 lb.) of butter. Blend to a smooth consistency.

Mint Butter   Add 90 mL (6 tbsp.) of finely chopped mint to 450 g (1 lb.) of butter. Blend this mixture well to a smooth consistency.

Onion Butter   Add 1 finely minced, small onion to 450 g (1 lb.) of butter. Blend to a smooth consistency.

Shrimp Butter   Add 360 mL (12 oz.) of puréed cooked shrimp to 450 g (1 lb.) of butter. Blend this mixture well to a smooth consistency.

Tuna Butter   Add 225 mL (8 oz.) of puréed canned tuna to 450 g (1 lb.) of butter. Blend this mixture well to a smooth consistency.

Salmon Butter   Add 225 mL (8 oz.) of puréed canned salmon to 450 g (1 lb.) of butter. Blend this mixture well to a smooth consistency.

Blue Cheese Butter   Add 120 mL (4 oz.) of puréed blue cheese to 450 g (1 lb.) of butter. Blend this mixture well to a smooth consistency.

Cheddar Cheese Spread

Approximate yield: 625 mL (2 1/2 cups)

450 g	(1 lb.)	old cheddar cheese, grated
10 mL	(2 tsp.)	Worcestershire sauce
10 mL	(2 tsp.)	onions, minced
1 mL	(1/4 tsp.)	tabasco sauce
5 mL	(1 tsp.)	vinegar
2 mL	(1/2 tsp.)	prepared mustard
180 g	(6 oz.)	cream cheese

Method

1. Place all ingredients in the mixing bowl of an electric mixer.
2. Blend at low speed until the mixture can be spread.
3. Store in the refrigerator until needed.

Avocado Spread

Approximate yield: 500 mL (2 cups)

2		ripe avocados, pitted, peeled and mashed
30 mL	(2 tbsp.)	onion, minced
1		clove of garlic, minced
10 mL	(2 tsp.)	lemon juice
5 mL	(1 tsp.)	chili sauce
		salt and pepper to taste

Method

1. Place all ingredients in the mixing bowl of an electric mixer.
2. Blend at low speed until the mixture can be spread.
3. Store in the refrigerator until needed.

Devilled Ham Spread

Approximate yield: 500 mL (2 cups)

375 mL	(1 1/2 cup)	ham, finely diced
20 mL	(4 tsp.)	onions, diced
5 mL	(1 tsp.)	parsley, chopped
15 mL	(1 tbsp.)	dry mustard
30 mL	(2 tbsp.)	mayonnaise
2 mL	(1/2 tsp.)	Worcestershire sauce
1 mL	(1/4 tsp.)	tabasco sauce

Method

1. Place all ingredients in the bowl of an electric food chopper.
2. Chop and blend until the mixture can be spread.
3. Store in the refrigerator until needed.

Sardine Spread

Approximate yield: 750 mL (3 cups)

625 mL	(2½ cups)	canned sardines, mashed
15 mL	(1 tbsp.)	onions, minced
15 mL	(1 tbsp.)	lemon juice
5 mL	(1 tsp.)	parsley, chopped
65 mL	(¼ cup)	mayonnaise

Method

1. Place all ingredients in the mixing bowl of an electric mixer.
2. Blend at low speed until the mixture can be spread.
3. Store in the refrigerator until needed.

Relishes

Carrot sticks   Peel and wash the carrots. Slice them into pieces 8 cm (3 in.) long and 6 mm (¼ in.) wide. Store the finished carrot sticks in ice water to keep them crisp.

Celery sticks   Wash the celery. Slice the celery into strips that are 8 cm (3 in.) long and 6 mm (¼ in.) wide. Store the finished celery sticks in ice water to keep them crisp.

Carrot curls   Peel and wash the carrots. Slice them paper thin lengthwise on a slicer. Roll up the thin carrot slices and secure them with toothpicks. Store the carrot curls in ice water to keep them crisp and to help them retain their shape. Remove the toothpicks before serving the carrot curls.

Radish roses   Use large, red radishes that are free from **blemishes.** Trim off the green stem and leaves to within 1 cm (½ in.) of the radish. Leave this small piece of stem on for colour contrast. Remove a thin slice from the opposite end of the radish. With a paring knife, cut five thin, verticle slices into the side of the radish. Do not cut completely off. Store the cut radish roses in ice water to keep them crisp and to allow the petals to open.

blemishes—flaws or defects

Find the Answers to These Questions

1. What is the purpose of an appetizer?
2. List the five categories of appetizers and give one example of each.
3. Why is crushed ice used with relishes?
4. Describe the main features of canapés.
5. Why is bread more versatile than crackers in the production of canapés?
6. What are vegetables à la grecque?

CHAPTER 7
STOCKS AND SOUPS

Watch for These Words

simmering   vigorously   roux
extraction   deglaze   enhances
virtually   procedures   garnishes
excessive   poaching   croutons
particles   hearty   sauté
accumulates   clarification   rendered

How to Use These Words

1. A __XXXX__ soup should be served before a light main course.
2. Boiling stock too __XXXX__ produces a cloudy stock.
3. Stocks are made by __XXXX__ bones and other ingredients.
4. We __XXXX__ the roasting pan with liquid to collect the caramelized drippings.
5. To __XXXX__, you cook something quickly in a small amount of fat.
6. Small pieces of toasted or fried bread used to garnish soups are known as __XXXX__.
7. If stocks are to be reduced, the addition of salt in the original stock would make them __XXXX__ unusable.
8. In the recipes included in this book, the __XXXX__ to be followed are listed under the heading "Method."
9. The bacon was sautéed until some fat was __XXXX__.
10. Bones used for making stock are cut in pieces to aid in the __XXXX__ of the flavour.
11. Equal parts of fat and flour which are cooked and used to thicken soups, sauces and gravies are called a __XXXX__.
12. __XXXX__ cooking of vegetables in a stock often results in a bitter-flavoured stock.

13. Foods used as decoration are known as __XXXX__.
14. Cheesecloth is used to strain all of the small __XXXX__ from a finished stock.
15. The use of garnishes __XXXX__ the appearance of soups.
16. __XXXX__ is the process of removing all the floating particles from a stock to leave a sparkling liquid.
17. Scum which forms on top of a simmering stock should be skimmed off as it __XXXX__.
18. A cooking method where fish is cooked in a lightly bubbling liquid is known as __XXXX__.

STOCKS

simmering—cooking just below boiling

Traditionally stocks are made by **simmering** bones, meat, poultry, fish, vegetables, herbs and spices in water for several hours. However, since this practice is time consuming, many establishments have switched to the use of prepared bases such as beef or chicken base. Whether or not a kitchen produces its own stocks or uses prepared bases, it is important for the professional cook to know the proper way to make stock from scratch. Since stocks are the basis for nearly all soups and sauces, they are a very important ingredient in food preparation.

extraction—taking out

virtually—almost

When preparing stocks, meat bones should be cut into usable sizes on the meat saw. The smaller the pieces, the more surface area of the bones is exposed. This makes the **extraction** of flavours easier. Stocks should never be salted. They are usually not used in their original form. If they are reduced or concentrated for use, the addition of salt in the original stock would make them **virtually** useless.

excessive—too much

Vegetables are added to the stock during cooking rather than at the beginning because **excessive** cooking destroys their food value and often results in a bitter-flavoured stock. A total cooking time for stock of five to six hours is normally sufficient to extract the desired flavours from the ingredients. Starchy vegetables such as potatoes should not be used in the preparation of stock. They make the stock cloudy. In addition, strong-flavoured vegetables such as cabbage and broccoli should not be used in stocks. The finished stock should have all solid particles removed by passing it through a fine sieve or cheesecloth. All fat should be removed either while the stock is still hot or by refrigerating the stock and then lifting off the solidified fat. While the stock is cooking, scum which forms on the top should be skimmed off as it **accumulates**. All stocks should be simmered and not boiled **vigorously**, as this produces a cloudy stock with limited usefulness. The proper method is to bring the pot to a boil and then reduce the temperature and simmer for the duration of the cooking time.

It is important that finished stocks should be cooled as quickly as possible for storage and to reduce the possibility of spoilage. A quick method of cooling stock is to place it in a sink with an overflow drain. The sink is then filled with cold running water to cool the stock. Excess water is taken off through the overflow drain. Occasionally stir the stock during this cooling process to allow the contents to cool more evenly and quickly. Once the stock is sufficiently cool, it can be refrigerated and stored for later use. Remember to always bring stock to the boil before using it.

There are four major stocks from which most soups, sauces and gravies are made. These are:

brown stock
white stock
chicken stock
fish stock

Brown stock is made from beef bones or a combination of bones, beef and veal for example. These are browned in the oven to provide added colour and flavour.

accumulates—collects
vigorously—energetically

RECIPES

Brown Stock   Approximate yield: 9 L (2 gallons)

5 kg	(11 lb.)	beef bones	
13.5 L	(3 gal.)	water to cover	
450 g	(1 lb.)	onions	
225 g	(8 oz.)	celery	mirepoix
225 g	(8 oz.)	carrots	
900 g	(2 lb.)	tomatoes	
2 mL	(½ tsp.)	thyme	
2		bay leaves	bouquet
3		parsley sprigs	garni
2 mL	(½ tsp.)	peppercorns, crushed	

mirepoix—mixture of onions, carrots and celery used for flavouring soups, stocks, sauces and stews

bouquet garni—herbs, usually parsley, thyme and bay leaf, tied in a bunch and used for flavouring soups, sauces, stocks and stews

Method

1. Cut the bones into usable sizes with a meat saw.
2. Brown the bones in a large roasting pan in the oven at a temperature of 190°C (375°F).
3. Turn the bones occasionally to allow for even browning.

deglaze—to moisten a roast pan with liquid in order to collect the caramelized drippings

4. Remove the browned bones to a stock pot.
5. **Deglaze** the roasting pan with part of the water.
6. Cover the bones in the stock pot with the water and the liquid from the deglazed pan.
7. Bring the pot to a boil and simmer for 3 h.
8. Sauté the vegetables for the mirepoix until they are browned.
9. Add the browned mirepoix, tomatoes, herbs and spices to the stock pot.
10. Simmer for another 3 h.
11. Strain the stock through a fine sieve or cheesecloth.
12. Cool and refrigerate.

White Stock

Approximate yield: 9 L (2 gallons)

5 kg	(11 lb.)	bones (beef, veal, chicken)
13.5 L	(3 gal.)	water to cover
450 g	(1 lb.)	onions
225 g	(8 oz.)	celery
225 g	(8 oz.)	carrots
2 mL	(½ tsp.)	thyme
3		parsley sprigs
2		bay leaves
2 mL	(½ tsp.)	peppercorns, crushed

Method

1. Cut the bones into usable sizes with a meat saw.
2. Wash and rinse the bones in cold water.
3. Place the bones in a stock pot and cover with the cold water.
4. Bring the stock pot to a boil and simmer for 3 h.
5. Add the mirepoix, spices, herbs and parsley sprigs.
6. Simmer for an additional 3 h.
7. Strain the stock through a fine sieve or cheesecloth.
8. Cool and refrigerate.

Chicken Stock

Approximate yield: 9 L (2 gallons)

5 kg	(11 lb.)	stewing chicken, chicken bones, necks and backs
450 g	(1 lb.)	onions
225 g	(8 oz.)	celery
225 g	(8 oz.)	carrots
13.5 L	(3 gal.)	water to cover
2 mL	(½ tsp.)	peppercorns, crushed
3		parsley sprigs
2 mL	(½ tsp.)	thyme
2		bay leaves

Method

Use the same **procedure** as for white stock.

procedure—method

Fish Stock

Approximate yield: 9 L (2 gallons)

5 kg	(11 lb.)	fish bones and trimmings
11 L	(2½ gal.)	water to cover
450 g	(1 lb.)	onions
225 g	(8 oz.)	celery
225 g	(8 oz.)	carrots
2 mL	(½ tsp.)	peppercorns, crushed
2		lemons, cut in quarters
2		bay leaves
3		parsley sprigs

Method

1. Place the fish bones and trimmings in the stock pot and cover with cold water.
2. Bring the stock pot to the boil and reduce heat to simmer.
3. Add the remaining ingredients and simmer for 30 min. (Extraction of flavours is much more rapid in the production of fish stock.)
4. Strain the stock through a fine sieve or cheesecloth.
5. Cool and refrigerate.

Essences and Glazes

Essences are obtained by boiling down stocks until they are reduced by one-half of the volume. Essences are used for adding flavour to sauces and for **poaching** fish.

Glazes are stocks that have been reduced until a thick and barely flowing liquid is produced. Glazes are used mainly for enriching and finishing sauces.

poaching—cooking in liquid that bubbles lightly

SOUPS

Soup is a liquid food made from the broth of meat, poultry, seafood or vegetables. Traditionally, soup was served as a complete, filling and nutritious meal. This is still true in some countries today. In North America today, soup is regarded as an appetizer which precedes the main course. A light soup should be served before a heavy main course and a **hearty** soup before a light main course. Most soups should be served piping hot in heated serving bowls. Exceptions to this are cold soups such as jellied consommés, vichyssoise, and gazpacho. These should be served in chilled bowls or cups.

hearty—robust and filling

classification—putting into groups

Since there is a wide variety of soups throughout the world, **classification** is difficult. To make learning about soups and their preparation easier, we will classify soups as:

> clear soups
> thick soups
> specialty soups
> cold soups

Clear Soups

Clear soups include bouillons, broths, consommés and vegetable soups. These clear soups are made with a rich, clear stock and are prepared without the addition of any starch or thickening agent. **Bouillons** and **broths** are much the same thing. They are made from the liquid in which any food has been simmered. They have a stronger flavour and are clearer than stocks. **Vegetable soups** are made from broths or bouillons which contain a variety of vegetables.

Consommés are sparkling, clear soups derived from stocks, bouillons or broths that have been clarified. They are reduced by simmering to provide a rich flavour of beef or poultry. A **clarification** process extracts all the floating particles from the stock, bouillon or broth to leave a stimulating and sparkling liquid.

clarification—the process of making clear

Thick Soups

Thick soups include cream soups, purées, chowders and bisques. Cream soups have been thickened with a **roux** and then completed by adding cream or milk.

Purées are soups that derive their thickness from the main ingredient in the soup. The main ingredients are usually starchy in nature and include dried beans, peas and lentils. These ingredients are cooked until they become pulpy and can be pressed through a fine sieve or food mill. Cream and milk should not be added to a purée.

Chowders are produced from fish, shellfish and vegetables. Although they usually contain cream or milk, they are distinguished from cream soups by the addition of diced potatoes.

Bisques are cream soups that are made from shellfish such as shrimp, crab and lobster.

roux—equal parts of fat and flour cooked together and used to thicken soups, sauces and gravies

Specialty Soups

These soups include a great variety of both clear and thick soups that have become identified with a particular coun-

A chowder soup makes a hearty meal. (Courtesy of the Ontario Ministry of Agriculture and Food)

try or region. Examples of specialty soups include mine-strone (Italy), oxtail (England), Scotch broth (Scotland), pot-au-feu (France), mulligatawny (India), Philadelphia pepper pot and New England clam chowder.

Cold Soups

These soups are favourites during the summer months. They may also be classified in some of the other groups of soups. Popular cold soups include vichyssoise, gazpacho, jellied consommés and cold bortsch.

Soup Garnishes

The use of appropriate garnishes greatly **enhances** the appearance of soups. Some **garnishes** are added to the soup when it is served, while others are added during cooking. Some garnishes commonly used with soups are cheese, **croutons**, chopped parsley, chopped chives, finely diced meats and poultry, noodles, tiny dumplings, sour cream, unsweetened whipped cream and vegetables cut in a variety of shapes such as **julienne, brunoise, paysanne** and **printanière**. In addition, crisp breads and crackers are usually served with soups. These include a variety of crackers, melba toast, bread sticks and large croutons.

enhances—improves
garnishes—edible decorations
croutons—small pieces of toasted or fried bread
julienne—cut in thin, matchstick slices
brunoise—cut in fine dice
paysanne—cut in square shapes
printanière—spring vegetables cut in small dice

Cold soups are favourites in the summer. (Courtesy of the Ontario Ministry of Agriculture and Food)

RECIPES

Clear Soups

sauté—cook quickly in a small amount of fat

French Onion Soup

Approximate yield: 4.5 L (1 gallon)

2.5 kg	(5½ lb.)	onions, peeled and sliced
120 g	(4 oz.)	butter
2.25 L	(2¼ qt.)	beef stock
2.25 L	(2¼ qt.)	chicken stock
		salt to taste
		pepper to taste

Method

1. Melt the butter in a soup pot over moderate heat.
2. **Sauté** the sliced onions in the butter until they start to brown.
3. Allow the onions to become evenly coloured without burning them.
4. Add the beef and chicken stocks.
5. Bring to a boil and reduce heat.
6. Simmer for about 45 min, until the onion flavour is well developed.
7. Remove any scum that appears with a ladle or skimmer.
8. Season with salt and pepper.

Vegetable Soup Approximate yield: 4.5 L (1 gallon)

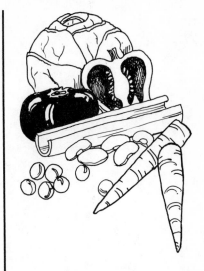

225 g	(8 oz.)	onions, diced
225 g	(8 oz.)	celery, diced
225 g	(8 oz.)	carrots, diced
120 g	(4 oz.)	cabbage, diced
225 g	(8 oz.)	peas
0.5 L	(1 pt.)	tomatoes, chopped
60 g	(2 oz.)	shortening
4.5 L	(1 gal.)	beef stock
		salt to taste
		pepper to taste

Method

1. Melt the shortening over moderate heat in a soup pot.
2. Sauté the diced onions, celery and carrots in the shortening until they are almost tender. Do not brown.
3. Add the stock. Bring to a boil and simmer for half an hour.
4. Add cabbage, peas and tomatoes and continue to simmer until all the vegetables are tender.
5. Season with salt and pepper.

Beef Consommé Approximate yield: 4.5 L (1 gallon)

450 g	(1 lb.)	beef shank meat, ground
360 g	(12 oz.)	onions, rough dice
225 g	(8 oz.)	celery, rough dice
225 g	(8 oz.)	carrots, rough dice
7 L	(1 ½ gal.)	beef stock, cold
4		parsley stems
1 mL	(¼ tsp.)	thyme
2		cloves
1		bay leaf
5 mL	(1 tsp.)	peppercorns, crushed
570 mL	(1 pt.)	tomatoes, canned
570 mL	(1 pt.)	egg whites

Method

1. In a stock pot add all ingredients except the egg whites and mix well.
2. Beat the egg whites slightly with a wire whisk and pour into the stock pot, stirring briskly.
3. Bring the stock pot to a slow boil, stirring occasionally.

4. Reduce the heat and simmer slowly until the coagulated mass comes to the surface.
5. Simmer for 1.5 h without breaking or disturbing the floating mass.
6. When the consommé is clear and full flavoured, strain it through fine cheesecloth.

Note: For chicken consommé, use the same recipe with chicken stock instead of beef stock. Omit the tomatoes and use 60 mL (2 oz.) of vinegar or lemon juice.

If the consommé is to be served cold as jellied consommé, add 120 mL (4 oz.) of unflavoured gelatin to each 4.5 L (1 gal.) of consommé. The gelatin should be soaked in cold water before adding it to the consommé.

Some Garnishes for Consommé

Breton	with julienne celery, leeks and onions
Brunoise	with cooked vegetables cut in small pieces
Célestine	with julienne of thin crêpes
DuBarry	with small flowerettes of cooked cauliflower
Florentine	with cooked spinach and julienne of thin crêpes
Julienne	with cooked vegetables cut in thin matchsticks
Printanière	with cooked spring vegetables cut in small pieces
Royale	with custard cut in various shapes

Vegetables to be used for garnishing consommé should be cooked in a small amount of consommé before they are served. When it is time to serve, a small amount of the garnish is placed in the serving dish and then the consommé is added.

Thick Soups

Cream of Mushroom Soup

Approximate yield:
4.5 L (1 gallon)

225 g	(8 oz.)	butter or margarine
225 g	(8 oz.)	onions, finely chopped
450 g	(1 lb.)	mushrooms, washed and finely chopped
180 g	(6 oz.)	flour
3.5 L	(3½ qt.)	chicken stock, hot
1 L	(1 qt.)	cream or milk, hot
1		bay leaf
		salt to taste
		pepper to taste

Method

1. Sauté the onions and mushrooms in the butter until soft. Do not brown.
2. Add the flour to make a roux and stir until all the flour is absorbed and smooth. Cook for 5 min.
3. Gradually add the hot chicken stock, whisking vigorously until the mixture is smooth and slightly thickened.
4. Add the bay leaf and simmer for 30 min until the vegetables are tender.
5. Remove the bay leaf and add the hot cream or milk.
6. Season with salt and pepper to taste.

Split-Pea Soup   Approximate yield: 4.5 L (1 gallon)

1		ham shank (if available)
675 g	(1 ½ lb.)	split peas, green or yellow
1		bay leaf
4.5 L	(1 gal.)	stock or water, hot
225 g	(8 oz.)	bacon, diced
450 g	(1 lb.)	onions, diced
225 g	(8 oz.)	celery, diced
90 g	(3 oz.)	flour
		salt to taste
		pepper to taste

Method

1. Place ham shank, split peas, bay leaf and 3 L (3 qt.) of stock in a stock pot and bring to a boil. Reduce to simmer.
2. Sauté bacon until some fat is **rendered**.
3. Add celery and onions and sauté until almost tender.
4. Add the flour to make a roux. Cook for 5 min.
5. Gradually add the remaining stock, stirring until it is smooth and slightly thickened.
6. Add the ham shank and split-pea mixture and simmer for 1 h until the split-peas are soft.
7. Remove the ham shank.
8. Pass the soup through a food mill and season with salt and pepper to taste.

rendered—melted and clarified

New England Clam Chowder

Approximate yield: 4.5 L (1 gallon)

3 L	(3 qt.)	fish stock and clam juice, hot
1.5 L	(1½ qt.)	cream and milk, hot
1 L	(1 qt.)	canned clams, drained and chopped
180 g	(6 oz.)	butter
180 g	(6 oz.)	flour
225 g	(8 oz.)	onions, diced
225 g	(8 oz.)	celery, diced
450 g	(1 lb.)	potatoes, peeled and diced
1 mL	(¼ tsp.)	thyme
5 mL	(1 tsp.)	Worcestershire sauce
		salt to taste
		white pepper to taste

Method

1. Melt the butter in a stock pot.
2. Add the diced onions and celery and sauté until almost tender. Do not brown.
3. Add the flour to make a roux and cook for 5 min.
4. Add the hot stock and clam juice, whisking it to make it smooth and slightly thick.
5. Add the potatoes, clams, thyme and Worcestershire sauce.
6. Simmer until the potatoes are tender.
7. Add the hot cream and milk slowly.
8. Bring the soup back to a simmer and season with salt and pepper.

Shrimp Bisque

Approximate yield: 4.5 L (1 gallon)

2.25 L	(2¼ qt.)	water	⎫
120 g	(4 oz.)	onions, finely diced	⎪
1		lemon, sliced	⎬ court bouillon
1		bay leaf	⎪
2		whole cloves	⎪
60 g	(2 oz.)	celery, finely diced	⎭
450 g	(1 lb.)	shrimp, raw	
225 g	(8 oz.)	butter	
180 g	(6 oz.)	flour	
5 mL	(1 tsp.)	paprika	
1.5 L	(1½ qt.)	milk and cream, hot	
		salt to taste	
		white pepper to taste	

court bouillon—a mixture of water and herbs in which fish is cooked

Method

1. Prepare a court bouillon by combining the water, onion, celery, lemon, bay leaf and cloves in a stock pot.
2. Bring to a boil and simmer for 15 min.
3. Strain the liquid into a soup pot and bring to a boil.
4. Add the raw shrimp and simmer for 7 to 8 min.
5. Remove the shrimp from the court bouillon and cool them in cold water.
6. Peel and devein the shrimp.
7. Chop the shrimp coarsely and set aside.
8. Melt the butter in a soup pot over moderate heat.
9. Add the flour and paprika to make a roux. Cook for 5 min.
10. Add the hot court bouillon slowly, whisking until it is smooth and slightly thickened.
11. Add the hot milk and cream.
12. Add the chopped shrimps.
13. Season with salt and pepper.

Specialty Soups

Minestrone Soup

Approximate yield: 4.5 L (1 gallon)

90 g	(3 oz.)	dried beans
3.5 L	(3½ qt.)	beef stock
60 mL	(2 oz.)	olive oil
60 g	(2 oz.)	kidney beans, canned and drained
120 g	(4 oz.)	chickpeas, canned and drained
450 g	(1 lb.)	onions, diced
225 g	(8 oz.)	celery, diced
225 g	(8 oz.)	carrots, diced
180 g	(6 oz.)	green peppers, diced
120 g	(4 oz.)	cabbage, diced
3 cloves		garlic, crushed and chopped
570 mL	(1 pt.)	tomatoes, canned and crushed
15 mL	(1 tbsp.)	parsley
2 mL	(½ tsp.)	basil
2 mL	(½ tsp.)	oregano
120 g	(4 oz.)	macaroni, cooked
		salt to taste
		pepper to taste

Method

1. Soak the dried beans overnight in water.
2. Drain and wash the soaked beans and cook in salted boiling water until tender.

3. Heat the olive oil in a soup pot.
4. Add the vegetables and garlic. Cover and cook until tender but not browned.
5. Add the stock, crushed tomatoes, basil and oregano.
6. Bring the soup pot to a boil and simmer for 30 min.
7. Add the cooked beans, kidney beans, chick peas, cooked macaroni and parsley.
8. Bring to a boil.
9. Season with salt and pepper.

Pot-au-feu

Approximate yield: 4.5 L (1 gallon)

1 kg	(2 lb.)	lean soup meat or boiling beef
4.5 L	(1 gal.)	cold water
450 g	(1 lb.)	carrots, cut in julienne style and tied in a bunch
4		leeks, white part only, tied in a bunch
360 g	(12 oz.)	turnip, cut in julienne style and tied in a bunch
360 g	(12 oz.)	celery, cut in julienne style and tied in a bunch
1		onion studded with four whole cloves
450 g	(1 lb.)	cabbage wedges, tied together
1		bay leaf
		salt to taste
		pepper to taste

Method

1. Place the soup meat in a stock pot and cover with the cold water.
2. Bring the pot to a boil and remove the scum.
3. Add all of the vegetables and the bay leaf.
4. Simmer for 2 to 2.5 h until tender. Remove any scum that accumulates.
5. Remove the meat and the vegetables from the bouillon.
6. Strain the bouillon and season with salt and pepper.
7. Serve the bouillon separately and place the vegetables neatly on a platter with the meat in the centre.

Cold Soups

Gazpacho Approximate yield: 4.5 L (1 gallon)

450 g	(1 lb.)	cucumbers
450 g	(1 lb.)	green peppers, chopped
450 g	(1 lb.)	onions, peeled
675 g	(1 ½ lb.)	tomatoes
3 cloves		garlic, crushed
225 mL	(8 oz.)	tomato purée
120 mL	(4 oz.)	vinegar
360 mL	(12 oz.)	olive oil
60 mL	(2 oz.)	lemon juice
570 mL	(1 pt.)	tomato juice
1 mL	(¼ tsp.)	cayenne
1 mL	(¼ tsp.)	cumin
1 mL	(¼ tsp.)	thyme
10 mL	(2 tsp.)	salt
1 mL	(¼ tsp.)	pepper

Method

1. Place all of the ingredients except the tomato juice in a food chopper.
2. Chop very finely until the ingredients are well blended and mixed.
3. Add the tomato juice and blend well with the other ingredients.
4. Adjust the seasonings and consistency, if required, and refrigerate the soup until well chilled.

Vichyssoise Approximate yield: 4.5 L (1 gallon)

120 g	(4 oz.)	butter
3 L	(3 qt.)	chicken stock
1.5 L	(1 ½ qt.)	cream
675 g	(1 ½ lb.)	potatoes, peeled and sliced
225 g	(8 oz.)	onions, diced
180 g	(6 oz.)	leeks, diced
1		bay leaf
120 g	(4 oz.)	celery, diced
2		white peppercorns
		salt to taste
		white pepper to taste

Method

1. Melt the butter in a soup pot.
2. Add the celery, onions and leeks and sauté in the butter until almost tender.
3. Add the stock, potatoes, bay leaf and white peppercorns.
4. Simmer until the potatoes are well done.
5. Pass the soup through a food mill and let the soup cool.
6. Add the cream and blend well.
7. Chill well before serving.

Find the Answers to These Questions

1. Describe a quick method for cooling stock.
2. List the four major stocks from which most soups, sauces and gravies are made.
3. What is the difference between an essence and a glaze?
4. How are soups classified?
5. List five garnishes used with soups.
6. Why should stocks never be salted?
7. What is the purpose of cutting meat bones into small, usable sizes when making stock?

CHAPTER 8
SAUCES

Watch for These Words

agent	imparts	bulk
proportions	curdle	reduction
granular	derivatives	
kneaded	blend	

How to Use These Words

1. The baker __XXXX__ the dough until the proper consistency was achieved.
2. If too much heat is used in the preparation of hollandaise sauce, the sauce will __XXXX__.
3. The __XXXX__ of mother or leading sauces are called small sauces.
4. A roux is a thickening __XXXX__.
5. A scorched sauce __XXXX__ a poor flavour to other foods.
6. When a roux is cooked, it should have a __XXXX__ texture.
7. The wine and herbs were simmered until a __XXXX__ was achieved.
8. __XXXX__ the ingredients together well.
9. The ingredients were mixed in equal __XXXX__.
10. The __XXXX__ of the sauce was scorched and what remained was of little use to us.

A sauce is a liquid dressing for meat, fish, poultry, desserts and other foods. Sauces should be smooth, have a definite flavour, be light in texture and have a glossy appearance. A gravy is also a sauce made from the juices of meat or poultry. A gravy always has the natural flavour of the meat that produced it.

THICKENING AGENTS

In the previous chapter we made reference to a **roux** as a thickening **agent** for certain soups. In addition to a roux,

agent—that which produces a reaction

there are several other thickening agents which may be used. These are cornstarch, beurre manié, whitewash, arrowroot and egg yolks.

Roux

A roux is a mixture of fat and flour, usually blended in equal **proportions**. The fat is melted, the flour is added, mixed and cooked until a moist, **granular** consistency is achieved. There are two main types of roux: light and brown. A light roux is used for thickening light or white sauces, while a brown roux is used to thicken brown sauces. The light roux requires only enough cooking to remove the raw starch taste. The brown roux requires longer cooking to produce the brown colour and some additional flavour. Bread flour is normally used to produce a roux.

Cornstarch

When cornstarch is mixed with a liquid and heated to thicken the liquid, it provides a glossy, semiclear finish. Cornstarch should be added to a small amount of cold liquid and blended until lump free and smooth. The liquid to be thickened is brought to the boil and the cornstarch mixture is added while stirring constantly to prevent scorching or the formation of lumps. Cornstarch is used mainly as a thickening agent for sweet sauces.

Beurre Manié

Beurre manié is a mixture of softened butter and flour which is **kneaded** until it is well blended. It may be made ahead of time and stored in the fridge. Small balls of beurre manié are dropped into sauce that is near boiling and mixed and cooked until the sauce is sufficiently thickened and smooth. Beurre manié is used to thicken small amounts of sauce quickly.

Whitewash

Whitewash is not recommended as a thickening agent. It is a mixture of flour and water which is added to a boiling sauce. It **imparts** no additional flavour and frequently causes lumps in the sauce if extreme care is not taken.

Arrowroot

As a thickening agent, arrowroot is used in the same way as cornstarch. The main difference is that arrowroot produces a much clearer sauce.

proportions—parts
granular—like small grains of sand

beurre manié—literally "handled butter"

kneaded—mixed and squeezed by hand

imparts—gives or adds

Egg Yolks

Egg yolks have to be used very carefully as a thickening agent. If they are subjected to too much heat, they will cause the sauce to **curdle**. Egg yolks are most effective when used in a **liaison**, which is a mixture of cream and egg yolks (three parts cream to one part egg yolk). This is added to soups and sauces to improve their flavour, colour and texture as well as to bind them together. A liaison is usually added to a sauce at the last minute to reduce the possibility of curdling.

The proper procedure for introducing a liaison into a sauce must be followed. The sauce is removed from the heat and small quantities are incorporated into the mixture of egg yolks and cream with a whisk. The addition of small quantities of sauce ensures that the temperature does not become high enough to curdle the egg yolks. When the **bulk** of the sauce is sufficiently cooled, the rest of the liaison mixture can then be added to the sauce. Egg yolks are also the thickening agent in hollandaise sauce and its **derivatives**.

curdle—congeal and coagulate

bulk—the major part

derivatives—those sauces made from hollandaise sauce

SAUCES

Although there is a large variety of sauces, they can all be classified as either warm sauces or cold sauces. The most numerous are the warm sauces, which may be served with

Warm sauces may be served with all types of food. (Courtesy of the Ontario Ministry of Agriculture and Food)

all types of food. Cold sauces are served with both cold and hot food. For the aspiring professional cook, the vast number of sauces need not be intimidating. Once the student has mastered five mother, or leading, sauces, he or she can prepare most other kinds of sauces.

Warm sauces are all derived from five mother sauces. The sauces derived from these mother sauces are called small sauces. The five mother or leading sauces are:

brown sauce (espagnole)
cream or white sauce (béchamel)
tomato sauce
velouté sauce
hollandaise sauce

RECIPES

Brown Sauce

Brown sauce is made from brown stock and a brown roux. It is the leading sauce from which many other sauces used with meat and poultry dishes are derived.

Approximate yield: 1 L (1 qt.)

60 g	(2 oz.)	fat
60 g	(2 oz.)	flour
1 L	(1 qt.)	brown stock, hot
30 g	(1 oz.)	tomato paste
120 g	(4 oz.)	carrots, rough dice ⎫
120 g	(4 oz.)	onions, rough dice ⎬ **mirepoix**
120 g	(4 oz.)	celery, rough dice ⎭
1		bay leaf
		salt to taste
		pepper to taste

blend—mix

Method

1. Melt the fat in a sauce pan.
2. Add the mirepoix and lightly sauté.
3. Add the flour to make a brown roux. Cook and stir until the proper consistency and colour are achieved.
4. Add the tomato paste and **blend** well with the roux.
5. Gradually add the hot stock, stirring constantly.
6. Add the bay leaf.
7. Bring to a boil and stir until the sauce is smooth and thickened.
8. Simmer the sauce for 2 h.
9. Add salt and pepper to taste and strain the sauce.

Sauces Derived from Brown Sauce

Demi-glace
Approximate yield: 1 L (1 qt.)

1 L	(1 qt.)	brown sauce
1 L	(1 qt.)	brown stock

Method

1. In a sauce pan, combine the brown sauce and brown stock.
2. Bring to a boil and stir until the sauce and the stock are well blended.
3. Reduce the heat to simmer and cook until the quantity is reduced by half.
4. Strain the sauce and store it for use in other sauces.
   This sauce is generally not served. It is reserved for use in other sauces.

Robert Sauce
Approximate yield: 1 L (1 qt.)

60 g	(2 oz.)	onions, finely chopped
225 mL	(8 oz.)	white stock
1 L	(1 qt.)	brown sauce
15 mL	(1 tbsp.)	dry mustard
30 mL	(2 tbsp.)	vinegar
60 g	(2 oz.)	butter

Method

1. Sauté the onions lightly in butter.
2. Add the dry mustard and blend well.
3. Add the white stock and reduce to one-half the original volume.
4. Add the brown sauce and vinegar and simmer for 30 min.
5. Finish the sauce by adding the butter and straining the sauce.
   This sauce is served with meats.

Mushroom Sauce
Approximate yield: 1 L (1 qt.)

225 g	(8 oz.)	mushrooms, sliced
60 g	(2 oz.)	onions, finely chopped
60 g	(2 oz.)	butter
1 L	(1 qt.)	brown sauce

Method

1. Lightly sauté the mushrooms and onions in butter without browning them.
2. Add the brown sauce and simmer for 30 min.
3. Remove from the heat and add the remaining butter.
   This sauce can be served with steaks, veal and meatloaf.

Chasseur Sauce   Approximate yield: 1 L (1 qt.)

120 g	(4 oz.)	mushrooms, sliced
60 g	(2 oz.)	onions, finely chopped
60 g	(2 oz.)	butter
1 L	(1 qt.)	brown sauce
2 mL	(½ tsp.)	dried tarragon
120 mL	(4 oz.)	tomatoes, canned and crushed
5 mL	(1 tsp.)	parsley, chopped
		salt and pepper to taste

Method

1. Sauté the mushrooms and onions lightly in butter. Do not brown.
2. Add the brown sauce, crushed tomatoes and tarragon and simmer for 10 min.
3. Add the chopped parsley and season to taste.
   This sauce is usually served with poultry.

Some Other Sauces Derived from Brown Sauce

Devilled sauce	onions, crushed peppercorns and cayenne added
Lyonnaise sauce	onions and parsley added
Italian sauce	onions, tomatoes, mushrooms and cooked ham added

Cream or White Sauce

Cream or white sauce is made with milk or cream and a light roux. It is a leading sauce from which many small sauces are made to accompany vegetables, fish, poultry and creamed dishes.

Approximate yield: 1 L (1 qt.)

60 g	(2 oz.)	butter
60 g	(2 oz.)	bread flour
1 L	(1 qt.)	milk or cream, hot
		salt to taste

Method

1. Melt the butter in a sauce pan.
2. Stir in the flour to make a roux. Cook over low heat, stirring constantly. Do not brown the roux.
3. Gradually stir in the hot milk or cream and whisk the sauce until it is smooth and thickened.
4. Bring the sauce to a boil and then simmer for 5 min.
5. Strain the sauce through a fine sieve.

Sauces Derived from Cream or White Sauce

À la King Sauce   Approximate yield: 1 L (1 qt.)

1 L	(1 qt.)	white sauce, hot
120 g	(4 oz.)	green peppers, diced
60 g	(2 oz.)	butter
90 g	(3 oz.)	mushrooms, diced
60 g	(2 oz.)	pimientos, diced

Method

1. Sauté the mushrooms in the butter until they are slightly tender.
2. Add the hot white sauce and simmer gently. Stir occasionally.
3. Poach the diced green peppers in a little water until they are tender.
4. Add the cooked green peppers and pimientos to the sauce.
5. Correct the seasoning if necessary.
   This sauce is used in the preparation of chicken or turkey à la king.

Mornay Sauce   Approximate yield: 1 L (1 qt.)

1 L	(1 qt.)	white sauce, hot
2		egg yolks
60 mL	(2 oz.)	cream
60 g	(2 oz.)	Gruyère (Swiss) cheese, grated
60 g	(2 oz.)	Parmesan cheese, grated

Method

1. Add the grated cheeses to the hot sauce and stir with a whisk until the cheese is melted and well blended.
2. Prepare a liaison by beating the egg yolks slightly and whisking in the cream.
3. Add small amounts of the sauce to the liaison and whisk them together gradually.

4. When the sauce is cool enough, add the rest of the liaison to the remaining sauce and slowly whisk it in.
5. Cook for about 1 min and remove from the heat.
   Do not overheat. If this sauce is overheated, the egg yolks will curdle and spoil the appearance of the sauce.
   This sauce is served with fish and vegetables.

Mustard Sauce   Approximate yield: 1 L (1 qt.)

1 L	(1 qt.)	white or cream sauce, hot
150 mL	(5 oz.)	prepared mustard
30 mL	(1 oz.)	white vinegar
		salt and white pepper to taste

Method

1. Add the mustard and vinegar to the hot sauce.
2. Simmer and whisk until the mixture is well blended.
3. Season to taste with salt and white pepper.
4. Remove the sauce from the heat.
   This sauce can be served with boiled ham, tongue or beef.

Cheese Sauce   Approximate yield: 1 L (1 qt.)

1 L	(1 qt.)	white or cream sauce, hot
225 g	(8 oz.)	cheddar cheese, grated
5 mL	(1 tsp.)	dry mustard
5 mL	(1 tsp.)	paprika
2 mL	(1/2 tsp.)	Worcestershire sauce
		salt and white pepper to taste

Method

1. Mix the dry mustard with a small amount of cold water.
2. Add the grated cheese, mustard and paprika to the hot white sauce.
3. Whisk until the cheese is melted and the ingredients are well blended.
4. Add the Worcestershire sauce and bring the sauce to a boil. Stir occasionally to prevent scorching.
5. Season to taste with salt and white pepper.
6. Remove from the heat and strain the sauce.
   This sauce may be served with vegetables such as asparagus, cauliflower and broccoli.

Some Other Sauces Derived from White or Cream Sauce

Cardinal sauce	cream and chopped shrimp or lobster meat added
Albert sauce	horseradish, onions and parsley added
Egg sauce	chopped hard-boiled eggs, chives and parsley added
Caper sauce	chopped capers added
Dill sauce	chopped fresh dill added

Tomato Sauce

Tomato sauce is a leading sauce used in the preparation of several small sauces.

Approximate yield: 1 L (1 qt.)

60 g	(2 oz.)	butter
5 mL	(1 tsp.)	garlic, finely chopped
120 g	(4 oz.)	onions, finely chopped ⎫
60 g	(2 oz.)	celery, finely chopped ⎬ mirepoix
60 g	(2 oz.)	carrots, finely chopped ⎭
60 g	(2 oz.)	flour
0.5 L	(1 pt.)	brown stock, hot
0.5 L	(1 pt.)	tomatoes, canned and crushed
300 mL	(10 oz.)	tomato purée
1 mL	(¼ tsp.)	thyme
1 mL	(¼ tsp.)	peppercorns, crushed
1		bay leaf
2		whole cloves
		salt to taste

Method

1. Sauté the chopped garlic in the butter until it is lightly browned.
2. Add the mirepoix and sauté until the vegetables are tender.
3. Add the flour to make a roux. Cook for 5 min.
4. Add the hot brown stock and whisk until the sauce is smooth and thickened.
5. Add the crushed tomatoes, tomato purée and the spices.
6. Simmer the sauce for 1.5 h.
7. Strain the sauce and season to taste with salt.

Sauces Derived from Tomato Sauce

Milanaise Sauce   Approximate yield: 1 L (1 qt.)

1 L	(1 qt.)	tomato sauce, hot
30 g	(1 oz.)	butter
60 g	(2 oz.)	mushrooms, sliced
60 g	(2 oz.)	tongue, cooked and cut in julienne style
60 g	(2 oz.)	ham, cooked and cut in julienne style

Method

1. Sauté the sliced mushrooms in the butter until they are tender.
2. Add the hot tomato sauce, tongue and ham and simmer for 15 min.
3. Remove from the heat and adjust the seasonings if necessary.
   This sauce can be served with pasta, veal and pork.

Napolitaine Sauce   Approximate yield: 1 L (1 qt.)

1 L	(1 qt.)	tomato sauce, hot
30 g	(1 oz.)	butter
2 mL	(½ tsp.)	garlic, minced
15 mL	(1 tbsp.)	parsley, chopped
1		tomato, skinned and diced
30 g	(1 oz.)	ham, cooked and diced

Method

1. Sauté the ham and the garlic in the butter.
2. Add the hot tomato sauce and simmer for 10 min.
3. Add the diced tomato and simmer for another 5 min.
4. Remove from the heat and add the chopped parsley.
   This sauce may be served with pasta, veal and pork.

Pizza Sauce   Approximate yield: 1 L (1 qt.)

750 mL	(3 cups)	tomatoes with juice, canned and crushed
300 mL	(10 oz.)	tomato paste
30 g	(1 oz.)	garlic, minced
30 g	(1 oz.)	onions, diced
120 mL	(4 oz.)	water
1 mL	(¼ tsp.)	pepper
10 mL	(2 tsp.)	basil
10 mL	(2 tsp.)	oregano
		salt to taste

Method

1. Combine the crushed tomatoes and juice, tomato paste and water in a sauce pot.
2. Bring to a boil and add the remaining ingredients.
3. Simmer and stir the mixture occasionally until it reduces slightly and becomes thick.
4. Adjust the seasoning if necessary.

Spaghetti Sauce   Approximate yield: 1 L (1 qt.)

60 mL	(2 oz.)	oil
120 g	(4 oz.)	onions, finely chopped
10 mL	(2 tsp.)	garlic, minced
30 g	(1 oz.)	celery, finely chopped
30 g	(1 oz.)	green peppers, finely chopped
750 mL	(3 cups)	tomatoes, canned and crushed
360 mL	(12 oz.)	tomato purée
2 mL	(1/2 tsp.)	basil
2 mL	(1/2 tsp.)	oregano
1		bay leaf
		salt to taste

Method

1. Sauté the onions, garlic, celery and green peppers in the oil for about 10 min. Stir frequently.
2. Add the crushed tomatoes and tomato purée and bring to a boil.
3. Add the basil, oregano and bay leaf and simmer for 2 h.
4. Pass the sauce through a food mill and season to taste with salt.

This sauce is used with pasta. For variety, cooked ground beef may be added for meat sauce or browned meat balls may be finished in the sauce for spaghetti and meat balls.

Some Other Sauces Derived from Tomato Sauce

Barbecue sauce	garlic, onions, sugar, mustard, vinegar, Worcestershire sauce and barbecue spice are added
Spanish sauce	onions, celery, mushrooms, garlic, tomatoes, green peppers and olives are added
Creole sauce	onions, garlic, green peppers and tomatoes are added

Velouté Sauce

Velouté sauce is a white sauce made with a white stock (white, chicken or fish) and a light roux. It is a leading sauce from which many small sauces are derived for use with poultry, fish and seafood.

Approximate yield: 1 L (1 qt.)

60 g	(2 oz.)	butter
60 g	(2 oz.)	flour
1 L	(1 qt.)	hot stock (white, chicken or fish)
		salt and white pepper to taste

Method

1. Heat the butter in a sauce pan.
2. Add the flour to make a light roux. Cook slowly for about 5 min.
3. Gradually add the hot stock and whisk constantly until the sauce is smooth and thickened.
4. Simmer the sauce for 20 min and season with salt and white pepper to taste.
5. Strain the sauce.

Sauces Derived from Velouté Sauce

Suprême Sauce
Approximate yield: 1 L (1 qt.)

1000 mL	(4 cups)	velouté sauce, hot
225 mL	(8 oz.)	whipping cream
		salt and white pepper to taste

Method

1. Heat the hot velouté sauce to simmer.
2. Gradually whisk in the whipping cream.
3. Season to taste with salt and white pepper.

This sauce can be used with poultry and fish or in the production of other sauces.

Poulette Sauce
Approximate yield: 1 L (1 qt.)

1 L	(1 qt.)	chicken velouté sauce, hot
30 g	(1 oz.)	butter
30 g	(1 oz.)	onions, minced
225 g	(8 oz.)	mushrooms, sliced
		salt and white pepper to taste

Method

1. Sauté the minced onion in the butter but do not brown.
2. Add the sliced mushrooms and continue sautéing until they are tender.
3. Add the hot velouté sauce and simmer for 15 min, stirring frequently.
4. Season to taste with salt and white pepper.
   This sauce is used with poultry.

Dugléré Sauce

Approximate yield: 1 L (1 qt.)

1 L	(1 qt.)	fish velouté, hot
30 g	(1 oz.)	butter
30 g	(1 oz.)	onions, minced
60 g	(2 oz.)	mushrooms, diced
60 mL	(2 oz.)	tomatoes, canned and crushed
10 mL	(2 tsp.)	parsley, chopped
		salt and white pepper to taste

Method

1. Lightly sauté the diced mushrooms and onions in butter.
2. Add the sautéed mushrooms and onions to the simmering velouté sauce and stir to blend well.
3. Add the crushed tomatoes and chopped parsley and stir to blend well.
4. Season to taste with salt and white pepper.
   This sauce is served with poached or baked fish.

Tarragon Sauce

Approximate yield: 1 L (1 qt.)

1 L	(1 qt.)	suprême sauce, hot
60 mL	(2 oz.)	white wine vinegar
45 mL or	(3 tbsp.)	fresh tarragon, chopped
10 mL	(2 tsp.)	dried tarragon
		salt and white pepper to taste

Method

1. Simmer the tarragon in the wine vinegar until it is reduced by one-half the original volume.
2. Add the hot suprême sauce and simmer for 2 to 3 min, blending well.
3. Season to taste with salt and white pepper.
   This sauce may be served with fish, chicken or eggs.

tarragon—an herb which is used in sauces, marinades and tomato juice

Some Other Sauces Derived from Velouté Sauce

parsley—a good source of
  vitamins A and C,
  iron and iodine

Parsley sauce	cream and chopped parsley are added
Anchovy sauce	cream and anchovy paste or finely minced anchovies are added
Horseradish sauce	horseradish and tabasco sauce are added

Hollandaise Sauce

Hollandaise sauce is a leading sauce from which several other small sauces are derived for use with fish, vegetables and eggs. Hollandaise is not a boiled sauce. Instead, it is beaten over moderate heat. The ingredients for hollandaise sauce are essentially butter and egg yolks. If the sauce is exposed to too much heat, the eggs will curdle the sauce.

Approximate yield: 1 L (1 qt.)

450 g	(1 lb.)	butter, melted
8		egg yolks
		the juice from half a lemon
		salt to taste
		cayenne to taste

Method

1. Mix the egg yolks with a few drops of water in a stainless steel bowl.
2. Place the bowl over a pot of simmering water like a double boiler. Do not let the bottom of the bowl touch the water.
3. Beat the egg yolks slowly with a whisk until they foam and soft peaks appear.
4. Remove the bowl from the heat.
5. Add the melted butter slowly, while whipping with a wire whisk.
6. When the sauce is thickened, add the lemon juice, salt and cayenne and blend well.

Sauces Derived from Hollandaise Sauce

Béarnaise sauce	a **reduction** of tarragon vinegar, crushed peppercorns and minced onion is added to the hollandaise
Mousseline sauce	whipped cream and hollandaise sauce are blended in equal proportions
Maltaise sauce	a reduction of orange juice and grated orange peel is added
Figaro sauce	an equal amount of tomato sauce is added

reduction—the result of simmering to make a smaller, more concentrated amount

Cold Sauces

Cocktail Sauce

Approximate yield: 1 L (1 qt.)

625 mL	(2½ cups)	chili sauce
450 mL	(1¾ cups)	ketchup
120 mL	(4 oz.)	horseradish
5 mL	(1 tsp.)	Worcestershire sauce
45 mL	(3 tbsp.)	lemon juice
1 mL	(¼ tsp.)	tabasco sauce
5 mL	(1 tsp.)	salt

Method

1. Combine all of the ingredients in a stainless steel bowl.
2. Blend well and chill.
   This sauce is usually served with seafood, both hot and cold.

Tartar Sauce

Approximate yield: 1 L (1 qt.)

750 mL	(3 cups)	mayonnaise
150 g	(5 oz.)	onions, finely chopped
300 g	(10 oz.)	dill pickles, finely chopped
30 g	(1 oz.)	parsley, chopped

Method

1. Combine all of the ingredients in a stainless steel bowl.
2. Blend well and chill.
   This sauce is served with seafood.

Rémoulade Sauce

Approximate yield: 1 L (1 qt.)

1000 mL	(4 cups)	mayonnaise
120 mL	(4 oz.)	prepared mustard
30 g	(1 oz.)	parsley, finely chopped
60 g	(2 oz.)	celery, finely chopped
60 g	(2 oz.)	capers, finely chopped
60 g	(2 oz.)	dill pickle, finely chopped
5 mL	(1 tsp.)	tarragon, dried
5 mL	(1 tsp.)	chervil, dried
3		anchovy fillets, mashed

Method

1. Combine all of the ingredients in a stainless steel bowl.
2. Blend well and chill.

This sauce is served with shellfish and grilled or broiled fish.

Find the Answers to These Questions

1. Name five thickening agents.
2. What are the two types of roux?
3. Why is whitewash not recommended as a thickening agent?
4. What precautions must be taken with a liaison?
5. Name the five mother sauces.
6. What is the difference between a white sauce and a velouté sauce?
7. What is a reduction?
8. What are the essential ingredients in hollandaise sauce?
9. Why is low heat used to produce hollandaise sauce?
10. List the mother sauce that each of the following sauces is derived from:
    a. Béarnaise sauce
    b. Demi-glace
    c. Mornay sauce
    d. Spanish sauce
    e. Tarragon sauce

CHAPTER 9
MEATS

Watch for These Words

modified	shrinkage	transmitted
evaporation	intense	reliable
conjunction	seared	wholesomeness
baste	calibrated	carcass

How to Use These Words

1. It is important to __XXXX__ the roast at regular intervals.
2. In braising, it is important that the meat be browned by __XXXX__ first.
3. When the student used a wet cloth to pick up the hot pot, the heat was __XXXX__ to his hands.
4. The __XXXX__ did not have a grade stamp evident.
5. The recipe was __XXXX__ to suit the tastes of the customers.
6. It is important to have __XXXX__ methods of testing meat for doneness.
7. The lower cooking temperature reduced the amount of __XXXX__ in the roast.
8. Braising uses a dry heat method of cooking in __XXXX__ with a moist heat method.
9. __XXXX__ heat is used for broiling meat.
10. Meat must be federally inspected for __XXXX__.
11. When making stews, boiling leads to rapid __XXXX__ of the liquid.
12. The roast was undercooked because the oven was not properly __XXXX__.

Meat is one of the main sources of **protein** in our diet. It is composed of muscle, connective tissue and fat. The muscle is the red part of the meat and consists of fibres known as the grain of the meat. The connective tissue is that white, stringy substance which encases the muscle fibres,

Roast lamb (Courtesy of the Ontario Ministry of Agriculture and Food)

holds them together and connects the muscle to the bone. The amount of connective tissue present in meat determines the tenderness of the meat. The more connective tissue present, the tougher the cut of meat will be. Less connective tissue means the meat is more tender.

Younger animals have less connective tissue in their meat than other animals. Thus, meat from young animals is more tender than meat from older animals. Fat appears in layers on the outside of the meat and also as small streaks within the muscle. These streaks of fat within the meat are known as **marbling**.

Because the amount of connective tissue varies in different cuts of meat, there are different methods of cooking the meat to produce a tender finished product. There are two basic methods for cooking meat. These are the **moist heat method** and the **dry heat method.** Both of these methods can be **modified** to provide for a variety of cooking procedures.

modified—changed slightly

MOIST HEAT METHODS

These methods are normally used for cooking the less expensive cuts of meat. These cuts contain more connective tissue. They require the use of moist heat to break down the connective tissue and make the cooked meat tender. Among the moist heat methods of cooking meat are:

    simmering
    steaming
    poaching

Simmering

The meat to be cooked is placed in a pot and covered with a liquid, usually water, and simmered until the meat is tender. Simmering is not boiling. Boiling produces vigorous action, with large bubbles and rapid **evaporation** of the liquid. The result of boiling is a stringy finished product. Simmering produces a gentle action of small bubbles which break below the surface of the water. It helps to protect the full nutritive value of the meat and to make it tender and less stringy. Simmering temperature is about 95°C (200°F).

evaporation—turning from a liquid into a vapour

Steaming

For steaming, use less liquid than with simmering. This method is mostly used in **conjunction** with other methods for cooking meat. Steaming may be carried out in a steamer unit, in a covered pot on the range, or in a pressure cooker.

conjunction—being together

Poaching

Poaching involves simmering in a small amount of liquid. Food items that are poached are seldom cooked to the well-done stage. Although poaching is a moist heat method of cooking, it is more commonly used in the preparation of items which do not require long cooking, such as eggs, fish and poultry.

DRY HEAT METHODS

Dry heat methods of cooking are used for the better cuts of meat, which have less connective tissue. These cuts become tender when cooked by dry heat methods. The dry heat methods are:

    sautéing
    pan frying
    roasting or baking
    broiling and grilling

Sautéing

This is a quick method of cooking thin, tender cuts of meat such as veal cutlets, pork tenderloin and beef tenderloin tips. The meat is fried lightly and quickly in a small amount of fat in a heavy-bottomed sauté pan. The meat is cooked uncovered.

rib of beef

baste—moisten with gravy or melted fat

shrinkage—becoming smaller

intense—high; very strong

T-bone steak

seared—having had the surface burned; scorched

Pan Frying

This method differs from sautéing in the amount of fat used. More fat is used in pan frying. This method is used for items that require a longer cooking time. Items are browned in a pan on top of the stove and then finished at a lower temperature in the oven.

Roasting or Baking

This is the process of cooking meat by surrounding it with dry, indirect heat in an oven. Little or no liquid is added to the meat. Meat to be roasted is placed with the fat side up in a shallow roasting pan and is cooked uncovered. Placing the meat fat side up ensures that the roast will continually **baste** itself during the roasting process. Meat should be roasted at temperatures between 150°C (300°F) and 180°C (350°F). Roasting meat at constant low temperatures instead of high temperatures provides a finished product that is more tender, juicy and flavourful. In addition, there are less **shrinkage** and higher yields because the meat is easier to carve.

Broiling and Grilling

Broiling means cooking meat by direct heat, either over hot coals or under gas flames. Only tender cuts of meat such as steaks and chops are cooked by this method. **Intense** heat is used and items are usually prepared to order. Grilling usually takes place on a solid grill, where the meat is not exposed to open heat. It is similar to sautéing.

METHODS COMBINING DRY HEAT AND MOIST HEAT

Braising

This method is used for cooking less expensive and tougher cuts of meat. The meat is first **seared** and browned on all sides in a little fat. A small amount of liquid, usually stock, is added and a simmering process continues in the oven in a covered brazier until the meat is tender. This cooking process breaks down the connective tissues of the meat and provides a flavourful sauce.

Stewing

Stewing is similar to braising. During the stewing process, meat is usually cut in small pieces. Meat to be stewed may or may not be browned, depending on the

Tender cuts of meat can be grilled. (Courtesy of the Ontario Ministry of Agriculture and Food)

desired colour of the finished product. Vegetables are added during the simmering process to provide a savoury and nourishing finished dish.

DETERMINING THE DEGREE OF DONENESS OF MEAT THAT IS ROASTED OR BROILED

As meat becomes well done, the amount of moisture present in it is reduced and the meat shrinks. Some meats, such as pork, must be cooked very thoroughly to kill the parasite trichina, which is present in pork. However, it is not necessary to overcook any meat to the point where it becomes dried out. Roasts that are cooked to the correct degree of doneness remain juicy and flavourful. There are several methods of determining the degree of doneness of meat. These are:

> the time-mass ratio
> the insertion of skewers
> the application of pressure with the fingers
> the use of a meat thermometer

In the **time-mass ratio** method, the meat is cooked for a specific number of minutes per kilogram. Charts are available which show the type and cut of meat, the degree of doneness required, and the number of minutes of cooking time per kilogram. For this method to be accurate, the oven temperature must be properly **calibrated**.

calibrated—have readings corrected or adjusted

skewer—a long pin of
wood or metal

The insertion of **skewers** determines doneness by checking the internal heat of the roast. A skewer is inserted into the meat at the thickest part of the roast. It is left for a few seconds and then withdrawn and placed against the cheek or some other sensitive area of the skin. The amount of heat **transmitted** to the skewer determines the degree of doneness. One drawback with this method is the loss of juices caused by piercing the meat with the skewer.

transmitted—passed on to

Applying pressure with the fingers to the largest portion of the meat is another way to determine the degree of doneness. If the meat is springy or more yielding to pressure, it is cooked to a lesser degree of doneness. The firmer or less yielding the meat is to finger pressure, the greater the degree of doneness. This method requires practice and experience and is not always **reliable**, depending upon the cut and quality of the meat. However, in broiling steaks and chops, it is the only reliable method of determining degree of doneness short of cutting into the meat.

reliable—able to be
depended upon

The most accurate method of determining the degree of doneness of meat is by the use of a **meat thermometer**. The thermometer is placed in the meat at the thickest part and away from any bone. As the meat cooks, its internal temperature is indicated on the thermometer. It is important to remember that a roast will continue to cook for a period of time after it has been removed from the oven. This factor should always be taken into consideration when roasting meats to particular degrees of doneness.

THE INSPECTION AND GRADING OF MEAT

Any meat crossing a border in Canada or into Canada must be inspected for **wholesomeness** by federal inspectors. Acceptable meats are stamped with a round purple stamp reading either "CANADA" or "CANADA APPROVED." This stamp is not an indication of the quality or grade of the meat but it does certify that the meat is safe for human consumption.

wholesomeness—
healthfulness

In Canada, grading of meat is voluntary except in those provinces that have grading laws. Grades are based on the texture and the colour of the flesh and fat and on the age of the animal that the meat comes from.

BEEF

There are four grades of beef. Each grade has a different coloured stamp which appears on the carcass in a continuous ribbon running the full length of the carcass.

These grades are:

    Canada A — red stamp
    Canada B — blue stamp
    Canada C — brown stamp
    Canada D — black stamp

Grade A beef, sometimes referred to as "red brand," has four subdivisions: A1, A2, A3 and A4. These subdivisions depend upon the level of fat present at a particular measuring point on the carcass. Grades B and C beef usually have less fat than Grade A beef. The colour of the fat and the lean may be somewhat darker than in Grade A beef. Grade D beef is generally less tender than the other grades because it comes from older animals. Although all grades of beef are wholesome and nutritious, cooking methods will vary depending on the grade. Most of the beef encountered in the commercial kitchen is either Grade A or B, since the dining public demands a certain level of quality.

RECIPES

Roasted and Baked Beef

Roast Prime Rib   Approximate yield: 25 portions

9 kg	(20 lb.)	roast ribs of beef, oven ready
450 g	(1 lb.)	onions ⎱
225 g	(8 oz.)	carrots ⎰ mirepoix, rough cut
225 g	(8 oz.)	celery ⎰
		salt to taste
		pepper to taste
2 L	(2 qt.)	beef stock, hot

Method

1. Place roast in roasting pan, fat side up.
2. Insert meat thermometer.
3. Roast at 180°C (350°F) for 2 h.
4. Add the mirepoix, salt and pepper.
5. Continue cooking until the meat thermometer indicates an internal temperature of 60°C (140°F) for rare or 65°C (150°F) for medium-cooked beef.
6. Remove the roast to a clean pan and hold in a warm place. (The roast should stand for about one-half hour before serving.)
7. Pour the fat off the roasting pan and deglaze the pan with the hot beef stock.
8. Simmer the mirepoix in the stock for a few minutes.
9. Strain the stock and reserve to serve with the roast beef.

Meat Loaf

Approximate yield: 25 portions

3.6 kg	(8 lb.)	medium ground beef
4		eggs
225 mL	(8 oz.)	milk
360 g	(12 oz.)	bread, without crusts
360 g	(12 oz.)	onions, finely chopped
225 g	(8 oz.)	celery, finely chopped
2 mL	(½ tsp.)	thyme
10 mL	(2 tsp.)	Worcestershire sauce
		salt to taste
		pepper to taste

Method

1. Sauté the onions and celery in a small amount of oil until tender.
2. Place the bread in a mixing bowl. Add the milk and mix well until the mixture is smooth.
3. Add the sautéed onions and celery, eggs, thyme, salt, pepper and Worcestershire sauce.
4. Add the ground beef and mix thoroughly.
5. Pack the mixture into greased loaf pans and bake at 180°C (350°F) for 1.5 h.
6. Remove the loaves from the oven, allow them to cool and refrigerate overnight.

Note: Meat loaf should be baked the day before it is to be served, since it slices much better when it is cold.

Braised Beef

Swiss Steak

Yield: 25 portions

25		bottom round steaks, 150 g (5 oz.) each portion
360 mL	(12 oz.)	vegetable oil
225 g	(8 oz.)	celery, sliced
450 g	(1 lb.)	onions, sliced
120 g	(4 oz.)	flour
2 L	(2 qt.)	brown stock, hot
1 L	(1 qt.)	tomatoes, canned and crushed
225 mL	(8 oz.)	tomato paste
		salt to taste
		pepper to taste

round steak

Method

1. Heat one-half of the oil in a large fry pan.
2. Brown the steaks on both sides and place them in a brazier or roast pan.
3. Heat the remaining oil in a sauce pan and sauté the celery and the onions for about 15 min.
4. Add the flour to make a roux and cook for 5 min.
5. Add the brown stock and stir until it is smooth and slightly thickened.
6. Add the tomatoes, tomato paste, salt and pepper and stir to blend well.
7. Pour the sauce over the steaks and bake at 180°C (350°F) for about 2 h, or until the steaks are tender.

Pot Roast of Beef   Approximate yield: 25 portions

5 kg	(11 lb.)	beef round or brisket
225 mL	(8 oz.)	vegetable oil
120 g	(4 oz.)	carrots, rough dice
225 g	(8 oz.)	onions, rough dice
120 g	(4 oz.)	celery, rough dice
225 g	(8 oz.)	flour
2 L	(2 qt.)	brown stock, hot
360 mL	(12 oz.)	tomatoes, canned and crushed
1		bay leaf
2 mL	(1/2 tsp.)	thyme
		salt to taste
		pepper to taste

brisket

Method

1. Heat the oil in a brazier. Add the meat and brown it on all sides in a hot oven.
2. Add the carrots, onions and celery and cook for 10 min.
3. Add the flour and stir to blend well with the fat. Cook for 5 min.
4. Add the hot brown stock and stir until the gravy is smooth and slightly thickened.
5. Add the tomatoes, bay leaf, thyme, salt and pepper and mix well.
6. Cover the brazier and simmer the pot roast in a 180°C (350°F) oven for 2.5 to 3 h until the meat is tender.
7. Remove the meat from the gravy and let it stand to cool slightly for ease of slicing.
8. Strain the gravy.

Beef Rouladen Approximate yield: 20 portions

2.25 kg	(5 lb.)	bottom round
450 g	(1 lb.)	bacon, diced
120 g	(4 oz.)	onions, diced
5 mL	(1 tsp.)	garlic, finely diced
225 g	(8 oz.)	ground beef
4		eggs, beaten
570 mL	(1 pt.)	bread crumbs
40		dill pickle lengths
2 mL	(½ tsp.)	marjoram
45 mL	(3 tbsp.)	paprika
		flour, salt, pepper to taste
120 mL	(4 oz.)	vegetable oil

Sauce:

2 L	(2 qt.)	brown sauce, hot
10 mL	(2 tsp.)	garlic, minced
450 g	(1 lb.)	onions, minced
225 mL	(8 oz.)	tomato purée
2		bay leaves
		salt to taste
		pepper to taste

bacon

Method

1. Slice the beef in 60 g (2 oz.) slices and flatten with a cleaver.
2. Combine the bacon, onions, garlic, ground beef, eggs, bread crumbs, marjoram and paprika in a stainless steel bowl and mix well.
3. Put one dill pickle length and 30 g (1 oz.) of the filling on each slice of meat.
4. Roll up the meat slices and secure them with toothpicks.
5. Dredge the meat rolls in the seasoned flour until they are well coated. Shake off the excess flour.
6. Brown the meat rolls on all sides in hot oil.
7. Place the meat rolls in a baking pan.
8. Combine all of the sauce ingredients and blend well.
9. Pour the sauce over the meat rolls and cover the pan tightly.
10. Braise in the oven at 180°C (350°F) until the meat is tender (about 1.5 h).
11. Strain the sauce, season to taste and serve over two rouladen per portion.

Beef stew (Courtesy of the Ontario Ministry of Agriculture and Food)

Beef Stew
Approximate yield: 20 portions

2.7 kg	(6 lb.)	boneless beef chuck, cut in 2.5 cm (1 in.) cubes
2.5 L	(2 ½ qt.)	brown stock, hot
225 mL	(8 oz.)	vegetable oil
225 mL	(8 oz.)	tomato purée
5 mL	(1 tsp.)	garlic, minced
225 g	(8 oz.)	flour
450 g	(1 lb.)	celery, large dice
450 g	(1 lb.)	carrots, large dice
675 g	(1 ½ lb.)	small whole onions, canned or frozen
450 g	(1 lb.)	green peas, frozen
2 mL	(½ tsp.)	thyme
2		bay leaves
		salt to taste
		pepper to taste

Method

1. Brown the beef cubes on all sides in hot oil in a brazier.
2. Blend in the flour to make a roux and cook slightly.
3. Add the hot brown stock, tomato purée, garlic, thyme and bay leaves. Blend with a kitchen spoon.

4. Cover the brazier and place it in an oven. Cook at 180°C (350°F) for about 2 h, or until the beef is tender.
5. Cook the vegetables in separate pots in boiling salted water until they are tender. Drain well.
6. When the meat is tender, remove the bay leaves and add the cooked vegetables.
7. Stir the stew to thoroughly blend all the ingredients.
8. Correct the seasoning and serve 225 g (8 oz.) portions.

Sautéed Beef

Beef Stroganoff   Approximate yield: 20 portions

2.25 kg	(5 lb.)	beef tenderloin tips
225 g	(8 oz.)	onions, finely diced
60 mL	(2 oz.)	vegetable oil
1.5 L	(1½ qt.)	brown sauce, hot
0.5 L	(1 pt.)	sour cream
450 g	(1 lb.)	mushrooms, sliced
120 g	(4 oz.)	dill pickles, diced
		salt to taste
		pepper to taste

Method

1. Cut the tenderloin tips in thin strips across the grain.
2. Heat the oil in a sauté pan and sauté the tenderloin tips until brown.
3. Remove the beef and set aside.
4. Sauté the onions until they are lightly cooked.
5. Drain off the excess oil.
6. Add the hot brown sauce to the onions and simmer.
7. Sauté the sliced mushrooms in a separate pan until they are tender.
8. Drain the mushrooms and set them aside with the beef.
9. Add the beef, mushrooms and dill pickles to the sauce and simmer for a few minutes.
10. Slowly add the sour cream and blend well.
11. Correct the seasoning and serve 150 g (5 oz.) portions.

LAMB

Lamb is the meat of young sheep, usually less than twelve months old. Lamb chops and roast leg of lamb are the most popular among lamb entrées. Some cuts of lamb are covered with a thin layer of membrane called fell. The fell is removed from chops but is usually left on legs and roasts of lamb to help retain moisture and shape during roasting. Lamb is highly perishable and should be carefully stored to avoid picking up foreign flavours and odours.

RECIPES

Roasted or Baked Lamb

Roast Leg of Lamb   Approximate yield: 20 portions

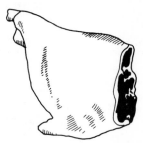

leg of lamb

2		legs of lamb 2.25 kg–2.7 kg (5-6 lb.) each, boned and tied
180 g	(6 oz.)	onions, rough dice ⎫
120 g	(4 oz.)	celery, rough dice ⎬ mirepoix
120 g	(4 oz.)	carrots, rough dice ⎭
1 mL	(1/4 tsp.)	garlic, minced
60 mL	(2 oz.)	oil
2 mL	(1/2 tsp.)	rosemary
180 g	(6 oz.)	shortening
120 g	(4 oz.)	flour
2 L	(2 qt.)	brown stock, hot
		salt to taste
		pepper to taste

Method

1. Place the legs of lamb in a roasting pan. Rub the lamb with the oil and season with rosemary, salt and pepper.
2. Roast until brown in a 190°C (375°F) oven. Add the garlic and the mirepoix. Reduce the temperature to 160°C (325°F) and roast until the lamb is done (70°C or 160°F internal temperature for medium), about 2 to 2.5 h.
3. Remove the lamb from the roast pan. Place in a bake pan, remove the twine and keep the meat warm.
4. Deglaze the roast pan with the brown stock.
5. Melt the shortening in a sauce pot.
6. Add the flour to make a roux. Cook for 5 min.
7. Strain the stock from the roasting pan into the roux. Stir with a wire whisk until the gravy is smooth and slightly thickened.
8. Simmer for 15 min.
9. Adjust the seasoning and strain the gravy.
10. Slice the roast lamb and serve in 90 g (3 oz.) portions with the gravy.

Broiled Lamb

Shish Kebab   Approximate yield: 20 portions

3.2 kg	(7 lb.)	leg of lamb, boned and cut in 2.5 cm (1 in.) cubes
40		small whole onions, canned or frozen
40		mushroom caps, lightly sautéed
40		cherry tomatoes or thick slices of tomato

Marinade:

1 L	(1 qt.)	vegetable oil
225 mL	(8 oz.)	vinegar
60 mL	(4 tbsp.)	lemon juice
2 cloves		garlic, minced
2 mL	(¹/₂ tsp.)	thyme
2 mL	(¹/₂ tsp.)	basil
2 mL	(¹/₂ tsp.)	oregano
5 mL	(1 tsp.)	rosemary
		salt to taste
		pepper to taste

Method

1. Blend all the ingredients for the marinade in a stainless steel bowl.
2. Add the lamb cubes and let marinate overnight.
3. Alternate food on metal skewers as follows:
     5 pieces of lamb
     2 tomatoes or slices of tomato
     2 mushroom caps
     2 onions
4. Cook the shish kebabs on the broiler for about 20 min over low heat.
5. Baste frequently with the marinade.
6. Serve the shish kebab over rice.

Broiled Lamb Chops   Yield: 20 portions

40		lamb chops, rib or loin, 150 g (5 oz.) each
225 mL	(8 oz.)	oil
		salt to taste
		pepper to taste

Method

1. Pour the oil into a baking pan.
2. Coat each lamb chop with the oil.
3. Season the chops with salt and pepper.
4. Brown the chops on one side in the broiler.
5. Turn the chops and brown on the other side.
6. Remove the chops from the broiler when they reach the desired degree of doneness.
7. Serve two lamb chops per portion.

Simmered Lamb

Lamb Stew   Approximate yield: 20 portions

3.2 kg	(7 lb.)	boneless lamb shoulder, cut in 2.5 cm (1 in.) cubes
3 L	(3 qt.)	water
450 g	(1 lb.)	whole onions, frozen or canned
900 g	(2 lb.)	potatoes
450 g	(1 lb.)	carrots, large dice
450 g	(1 lb.)	turnip, large dice
225 g	(8 oz.)	shortening
180 g	(6 oz.)	flour
120 g	(4 oz.)	leeks, finely chopped
5 mL	(1 tsp.)	marjoram
		salt to taste
		pepper to taste

Method

1. Cover the lamb cubes with the water in a stock pot.
2. Bring to a boil and skim off any scum that comes to the surface.
3. Add the marjoram and simmer until the lamb is slightly tender.
4. Cook the onions, potatoes, carrots and turnip in boiling, salted water in separate pots.
5. Melt the shortening in a sauce pot. Add the flour to make a roux and cook for a few minutes. Do not brown.
6. When the lamb is cooked, strain the cooking liquid into the roux. Stir with a wire whisk until the sauce is thick and smooth.
7. Add the lamb, the leeks and the cooked vegetables.
8. Simmer for a few minutes, stirring occasionally.
9. Adjust the seasonings and serve in 225 g (8 oz.) portions.

Curried Lamb
Approximate yield: 20 portions

3.2 kg	(7 lb.)	boneless lamb shoulder, cut in 2.5 cm (1 in.) cubes
3 L	(3 qt.)	water
450 g	(1 lb.)	onions, finely diced
450 g	(1 lb.)	apples, diced
360 g	(12 oz.)	shortening
225 g	(8 oz.)	flour
15 mL	(1 tbsp.)	curry powder
2		bay leaves
2 mL	(1/2 tsp.)	marjoram
1 mL	(1/4 tsp.)	ground cloves
		salt to taste
		pepper to taste

Method

1. Place the lamb in a stock pot. Cover with the water and bring to a boil.
2. Remove any scum that comes to the surface.
3. Add the bay leaves and the marjoram. Simmer until the lamb is tender.
4. Melt the shortening in a sauce pan. Sauté the onions until they are tender.
5. Add the flour and the curry powder to make a roux. Blend well and cook for 5 min.
6. Strain the hot stock from the cooked lamb into the roux and stir with a wire whisk until the sauce is smooth and slightly thickened.
7. Add the diced apples and ground cloves and simmer the sauce for 30 min.
8. Strain the sauce and add the cooked cubes of lamb. Blend well with the sauce.
9. Correct the seasonings and serve 225 g (8 oz.) portions over rice.

Braised Lamb

Navarin of Lamb
Approximate yield: 20 portions

3.2 kg	(7 lb.)	boneless lamb shoulder, cut in 2.5 cm (1 in.) cubes
225 mL	(8 oz.)	oil
2 L	(2 qt.)	brown stock, hot
225 g	(8 oz.)	flour
2		bay leaves
5 mL	(1 tsp.)	marjoram
450 g	(1 lb.)	small whole onions, canned or frozen

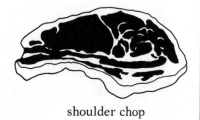

shoulder chop

450 g	(1 lb.)	carrots, sliced
450 g	(1 lb.)	turnips, large dice
1 L	(1 qt.)	tomatoes, canned and drained
		salt to taste
		pepper to taste

Method

1. Heat the oil in a brazier.
2. Add the cubes of lamb and brown thoroughly.
3. Add the flour and blend well to make a roux. Cook for 5 min.
4. Add the brown stock and stir constantly until the sauce becomes smooth and slightly thickened.
5. Add the bay leaves and marjoram. Cover the brazier and cook in a 180°C (350°F) oven until the lamb is tender.
6. Cook the onions, carrots and turnips in boiling salted water in separate pots until the vegetables are barely tender.
7. Add the drained vegetables and the tomatoes to the lamb.
8. Bring the stew to a boil and adjust the seasonings.
9. Serve in 225 g (8 oz.) portions.

PORK

Pork is the meat of young hogs, usually less than twelve months old. It is marketed in many different forms, including fresh, cured and smoked and salted. Pork is a popular menu item with Canadians. It is highly perishable in its fresh form and should be stored at temperatures between 0.6°C (33°F) and 3.3°C (38°F).

Pork must be cooked well done to destroy the parasite which causes trichinosis. An internal temperature of 76°C (170°F) is sufficient to make sure that pork is safe to eat.

RECIPES

Roasted or Baked Pork

Roast Pork Loin　　　　　Approximate yield: 20 portions

7 kg	(15 lb.)	pork loin
120 g	(4 oz.)	celery, rough dice
225 g	(8 oz.)	onions, rough dice } mirepoix
120 g	(4 oz.)	carrots, rough dice
120 g	(4 oz.)	flour
2 L	(2 qt.)	brown stock, hot
		salt to taste
		pepper to taste

loin rib roast

Method

1. Season the pork loin with salt and pepper.
2. Place the pork loin, fat side up, in a roast pan.
3. Roast at 190°C (375°F) until the meat is browned.
4. Reduce the oven temperature to 160°C (325°F). Remove the excess fat from the roasting pan and save for later use in the gravy.
5. Add the mirepoix and continue to roast until the pork is well done (internal temperature of 76°C or 170°F).
6. Remove the roast pork loin and keep warm.
7. Pour fat from the roasting pan and deglaze the pan with the brown stock.
8. Heat the reserved pork fat in a sauce pan.
9. Add the flour to make a roux and cook for 5 min.
10. Add the stock from the roast pan to the roux. Stir with a wire whisk until the gravy is smooth and slightly thickened. Simmer the gravy for 30 min.
11. Adjust the seasonings, if necessary, and strain the gravy.
12. Slice the roast pork loin and serve with the gravy.

Barbecued Spareribs   Yield: 20 portions

20 pieces		pork spareribs, cut in 360 g (12 oz.) portions
0.5 L	(1 pt.)	oil
1.5 L	(1½ qt.)	barbecue sauce (See Chapter 8.)

Method

1. Place the spareribs in a large stock pot. Cover with boiling water.
2. Simmer for 30 min.
3. Remove the ribs from the water and place on sheet pans.
4. Lightly oil the spareribs and brown both sides on the broiler.
5. Place the browned ribs in a roasting pan with the inside of the rib down.
6. Cover the spareribs with barbecue sauce and bake in the oven at 180°C (350°F) for 1 to 1.5 h until the ribs are tender.
7. Baste the ribs occasionally and turn them once during cooking.
8. Serve one 360 g (12 oz.) piece per portion.

Braised Pork

Braised Pork Chops Creole   Yield: 20 portions

20		loin pork chops, 150 g (5 oz.) each
2 L	(2 qt.)	Creole sauce (See Chapter 8.)
450 g	(1 lb.)	flour
15 mL	(1 tbsp.)	salt
2 mL	(1/2 tsp.)	pepper
0.5 L	(1 pt.)	oil

Method

1. Heat the oil in a fry pan.
2. Coat each pork chop lightly with seasoned flour. Shake off excess flour.
3. Brown the pork chops on both sides in the hot oil.
4. Remove the chops from the fry pan.
5. Place the browned pork chops in a baking pan and cover with the Creole sauce.
6. Bake in a 180°C (350°F) oven until the chops are tender.
7. Serve one chop per portion with Creole sauce.

Sautéed Pork

Breaded Pork Cutlet   Yield: 20 portions

20		boneless pork loin chops, 120 g (4 oz.) each
225 g	(8 oz.)	flour
15 mL	(1 tbsp.)	salt
2 mL	(1/2 tsp.)	pepper
3		whole eggs, beaten
1 L	(1 qt.)	milk
1 L	(1 qt.)	bread crumbs
360 g	(12 oz.)	shortening

Method

1. Flatten each cutlet slightly with a mallet or the flat side of a cleaver.
2. Prepare the ingredients for the breading procedure.
   a) Place the flour in a bake pan and season with salt and pepper.
   b) Beat the eggs with a wire whisk and add the milk to make an egg wash.
   c) Place the bread crumbs in a bake pan.
3. Pass each cutlet through the seasoned flour to coat it completely. Shake off excess flour.

To bread food, dip it in flour, then in eggwash, and finally in the crumb mixture.

4. Place the cutlets in the egg wash.
5. Remove the cutlets from the egg wash and place them in the bread crumbs.
6. Press each cutlet firmly to coat it completely with bread crumbs. Shake off excess crumbs.
7. Heat the shortening in a fry pan.
8. Brown the cutlets on one side and then turn to finish cooking on the other side.
9. When the cutlets are cooked to a golden brown, remove them from the pan and allow them to drain.
10. Serve one cutlet per portion with a mushroom or tomato sauce.

Broiled Pork

Ham Steak Hawaiian
Yield: 20 portions

20		ham steaks, 120 g (4 oz.) each
		oil
20		pineapple slices
20		maraschino cherries
		butter
120 g	(4 oz.)	sugar
2 mL	(1/2 tsp.)	cinnamon

Method

1. Place the ham steaks on a lightly oiled sheet pan.
2. Lightly brown the ham steaks under the broiler for about 3 min on each side.

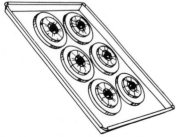

3. Remove the ham steaks from the broiler and keep warm.
4. Place the pineapple slices on a lightly buttered sheet pan.
5. Combine the sugar with the cinnamon and sprinkle over the pineapple rings.
6. Place the pineapple under the broiler and melt the sugar until the rings are glazed.
7. Before serving, place one pineapple ring on each ham steak. Place one maraschino cherry in the centre of each pineapple ring.

VEAL

Veal is the meat of milk-fed calves which are usually not over twelve weeks of age. Veal has very little fat covering. If veal is cooked too long or at too high a temperature it will become dry. Veal is the most delicate of all the meats. It blends well with other foods and can be served with many savoury sauces.

RECIPES

Braised Veal

Hungarian Goulash   Approximate yield: 20 portions

3.2 kg	(7 lb.)	boneless veal, cut in 2.5 cm (1 in.) cubes
225 mL	(8 oz.)	oil
900 g	(2 lb.)	onions, finely diced
180 g	(6 oz.)	flour
30 g	(1 oz.)	paprika
2		bay leaves
5 mL	(1 tsp.)	caraway seeds
2.5 L	(2½ qt.)	brown stock, hot
360 mL	(12 oz.)	tomato purée
		salt to taste
		pepper to taste
0.5 L	(1 pt.)	sour cream

Method
1. Heat the oil in a brazier.
2. Add the cubed veal and diced onions and sauté until the onions are tender.
3. Add the paprika and blend well.
4. Add the flour to make a roux and cook for 5 min.
5. Add the bay leaves, caraway seeds, brown stock and tomato purée.

6. Bring to a boil, cover the brazier and finish cooking in a 180°C (350°F) oven for about 1 h, or until tender.
7. Remove from the oven and adjust the seasoning if necessary.
8. Serve in 120 g (4 oz.) portions over noodles with sour cream on the side.

Osso Bucco   Yield: 20 portions

40		pieces of veal shank, cut in 5 cm (2 in.) lengths across the bone
450 g	(1 lb.)	flour
15 mL	(1 tbsp.)	salt
2 mL	(½ tsp.)	pepper
360 mL	(12 oz.)	oil
2		garlic cloves
450 g	(1 lb.)	onions, finely diced
180 g	(6 oz.)	flour
2 L	(2 qt.)	brown stock
120 g	(4 oz.)	tomato purée
225 mL	(8 oz.)	white stock
30 mL	(2 tbsp.)	parsley, chopped
15 mL	(1 tbsp.)	lemon rind, grated
		salt to taste
		pepper to taste

Method

1. Place the 450 g (1 lb.) of flour in a bake pan and season with salt and pepper.

dredge—sprinkle or dust with flour

2. **Dredge** the veal shanks in the seasoned flour and shake off the excess.
3. Heat the oil in a brazier.
4. Brown the veal shanks in the hot oil.
5. Remove the veal shanks from the brazier.
6. Sauté the garlic and the onions in the oil used to brown the veal shanks.
7. Add the 180 g (6 oz.) of flour to make a roux. Cook for 5 min.
8. Add the brown stock, tomato purée and white stock to the roux. Stir with a wire whisk until the sauce is smooth and slightly thickened.
9. Put the browned veal shanks in the brazier with the sauce. Cover and bake in a 180°C (350°F) oven for about 1 h until the meat is tender.
10. Add the chopped parsley and grated lemon rind. Simmer for 5 min. Adjust the seasonings.

11. Serve two shanks with sauce per portion with rice or pasta.

Simmered Veal

Veal Fricassee   Approximate yield: 20 portions

3.2 kg	(7 lb.)	boneless veal shoulder, cut in 2.5 cm (1 in.) cubes
3 L	(3 qt.)	water
2 mL	(1/2 tsp.)	thyme
1		bay leaf } bouquet garni
60 g	(2 oz.)	parsley
2 mL	(1/2 tsp.)	peppercorns, crushed
450 g	(1 lb.)	small onions, canned or frozen
450 g	(1 lb.)	mushrooms, sliced
30 mL	(1 oz.)	lemon juice
60 g	(2 oz.)	butter
225 g	(8 oz.)	shortening
225 g	(8 oz.)	flour
		veal stock, from cooking the cubed veal
		salt to taste

Method

1. Place the 3 L of water in a stock pot with the veal and bring to a boil.
2. Add the bouquet garni and simmer for 1.5 h. Skim off scum on the surface of the stock as it appears.
3. If the onions are frozen, cook in boiling, salted water until they are tender.
4. Sauté the sliced mushrooms in the butter and lemon juice until they are tender.
5. In a sauce pot, melt the shortening and add the flour to make a roux. Cook for 5 min but do not brown the roux.
6. When the veal is cooked, remove the meat from the stock. Remove the bouquet garni.
7. Add the veal stock to the roux and stir until the sauce is smooth and slightly thickened.
8. Season with salt.
9. Add the cooked veal, onions and mushrooms to the sauce and blend well.
10. Serve 225 g (8 oz.) portions.

Sautéed Veal

Breaded Veal Cutlet

Yield: 20 portions

20		pieces of boneless leg of veal, sliced 6 mm (¼ in.) thick
225 g	(8 oz.)	flour
15 mL	(1 tbsp.)	salt
2 mL	(½ tsp.)	pepper
3		eggs, whole, beaten
1 L	(1 qt.)	milk
1 L	(1 qt.)	bread crumbs
180 mL	(6 oz.)	oil

Method

1. Use a mallet to slightly flatten the veal cutlets.
2. Bread the cutlets according to the breading procedure outlined on pages 111 and 112.
3. Heat the oil in a sauté pan and sauté the cutlets until they are golden brown on one side.
4. Turn the cutlets and brown on the other side.
5. Remove the cutlets from the pan and drain well.
6. Serve one cutlet per portion.

Sautéed Veal Chops

Yield: 20 portions

20		veal chops, loin or rib, cut in 180 g (6 oz.) portions
450 g	(1 lb.)	flour
		salt to taste
		pepper to taste
360 g	(12 oz.)	shortening

Method

1. Place the flour in a bake pan and season with salt and pepper.
2. Melt the shortening in a sauté pan.
3. Dredge each veal chop in the seasoned flour until completely coated. Shake off the excess flour.
4. Sauté the coated chops in the hot shortening until one side is golden brown.
5. Turn the chops and brown the other side.
6. Remove the chops and drain well.
7. Serve one chop per portion with an appropriate sauce, for example a mushroom or Spanish sauce.

VARIETY MEATS

Variety meats include liver, brains, heart, tongue, kidneys, tripe and sweetbreads. They are excellent sources of vitamins and minerals. Variety meats are more perishable than other meats. Thus, they should be cooked and served as soon after purchase as possible.

Liver (Beef, Veal, Pork and Lamb)

Beef liver is the largest and least tender of the livers. Veal liver comes from milk-fed calves and is very flavourful and tender. Calf liver comes from older calves that are not milk fed. It is the most popular of the livers because of its tenderness and flavour. Pork liver is less tender and has a stronger flavour than other livers. Lamb liver is milder in flavour than either beef or pork liver.

The veal, calf and lamb livers are suitable for pan frying, broiling and sautéing, while beef and pork livers are best when they are braised.

Brains (Beef, Veal, Pork and Lamb)

Brains are inexpensive and simple to prepare. Before cooking, they should be soaked in cold, salted water for 30 min and then drained. Next they should be covered with boiling, salted water with a little lemon juice in it. Simmer the brains for 30 min, drain and plunge them into cold water. The thin membrane surrounding the brains can then be peeled off before the meat is used in a recipe.

Heart (Beef, Veal, Pork and Lamb)

Heart is one of the less tender meats. It requires long, slow and moist cooking. Beef heart requires about three hours of cooking time, while veal, pork and lamb hearts can be cooked in approximately two hours.

Tongue (Beef, Veal, Pork and Lamb)

Tongue is usually available fresh, pickled, corned or smoked. Pickled or smoked tongue may have to be soaked in fresh water for several hours to tone down its strong flavour. Tongue is usually simmered in water to which vegetables, spices and seasonings have been added. Three to four hours is the normal cooking time. After cooking, the tongue is skinned and any bones at the base are removed. Tongue can be served hot or cold.

Kidneys (Beef, Veal, Pork and Lamb)

Beef kidneys are the least tender of the group and are best cooked by braising. Veal, pork and lamb kidneys are tender enough to be broiled.

Tripe (Beef)

Tripe is the lining of a beef stomach. The honeycomb type is from the second stomach and is more tender and delicate than the smooth tripe, which comes from the first stomach. Tripe should be precooked prior to further preparation. Simmer the tripe slowly for 2 h in salted water to which herbs and spices may be added.

Sweetbreads (Veal and Lamb)

Sweetbreads are the thymus glands of young beef and lamb. As the animal grows, the gland disappears. What is sometimes marketed as a sweetbread is actually the pancreas, which is a much larger and softer organ. Before being used in any recipe, sweetbreads should be **parboiled** in the same manner as brains.

parboiled—boil and partly cook

Find the Answers to These Questions

1. What are the three components of meat?
2. What determines tenderness in meat?
3. List the moist heat methods of cooking meat.
4. Describe the difference between sautéing and pan frying.
5. Which is the most accurate method of determining how well done a piece of meat is?
6. What cooking methods are used for each of the following:
   a. pot roast of beef
   b. beef stroganoff
   c. shish kebab
   d. curried lamb
   e. veal fricassee
7. Why must pork be cooked very thoroughly?

CHAPTER 10
POULTRY

Watch for These Words

complex
deformities
perish
succulent

How to Use These Words

1. If poultry is not properly stored, it will __XXXX__ very quickly.
2. The roast chicken was moist and __XXXX__ .
3. The student advanced from simple to more __XXXX__ preparations.
4. Grade A poultry cannot have any __XXXX__ .

Domestic birds that are bred and sold for human consumption are **classified** as poultry. Included in this classification are chicken, turkey, duck, goose, squab and Rock Cornish game hen. Wild birds are usually hunted for sport and may then be used for food. These birds are classified as game birds. Included in this classification are such wild birds as grouse, pheasant, partridge, quail and wild ducks.

Poultry is rich in protein, vitamins and minerals. It is easily digestible because of its short meat fibres. Poultry is readily available and can be prepared in a great variety of ways ranging from fairly simple to more **complex** preparations.

classify—to put in a particular class

complex—complicated

GRADING OF POULTRY

In Canada, national grading regulations control the import, export and the interprovincial movement of all poultry. The grade mark for poultry is normally found on a metal tag attached to the breast skin of the bird or, in the case of frozen poultry, printed on the wrapping in which the poultry is encased.

The highest grade, Canada Grade Special (purple) is reserved for the finest, most perfect birds. Grade A (red) poultry have no deformities and are fat and well fleshed. Grade B (blue) birds may have some slight **deformities**, less fat and flesh than Grade A birds, and they may have some skin tears which do not seriously detract from the overall appearance of the bird. Canada Grade Utility (blue) are Grade B birds with one or more parts missing. These parts, such as a wing or a drumstick, are usually missing because of some problem during processing. Utility grade birds are a good buy if the bird is going to be cut into pieces before cooking or if the meat is to be removed and used in a recipe. Canada Grade C (yellow) are birds which have large skin tears and noticeable discolouration. These birds usually are processed for canning. Turkeys, geese and ducks must also have the designation "young" or "mature" on a grade tag.

TYPES OF POULTRY

Fryers and Broilers

These are young chickens, six to ten weeks of age. They are very tender and range in mass from 675 g (1 1/2 lb.) to 1.6 kg (3 1/2 lb.).

Roasters

These are tender chickens from ten weeks to seven months old. The average mass of roasters is from 1.4 kg (3 lb.) to 2.2 kg (5 lb.).

Capons

Capons are castrated male chickens, five to nine months old. They are very tender and have good fat covering, with a high proportion of light meat. The average mass of capons is from 2.2 kg (5 lb.) to 3.6 kg (8 lb.). These birds are suitable for roasting.

Fowl

These are mature hens over seven months old. They are also referred to as stewing chickens. The flesh and skin are quite tough. They are usually cooked by moist heat methods to produce meat tender enough for use in such preparations as chicken salad and chicken à la king. The average mass of fowl is between 1.8 kg (4 lb.) and 2.7 kg (6 lb.).

Roast turkey (Courtesy of the Ontario Ministry of Agriculture and Food)

Turkey

Turkey may be purchased as broilers, which are under fifteen weeks in age and under 4.5 kg (10 lb.) in mass. Young hens (females) are usually seventeen to eighteen weeks old and have a mass of 4.5 to 7.2 kg (10 to 16 lb.). Young toms (males) are between twenty and twenty-six weeks of age. They have a mass of over 7.2 kg (16 lb.).

Squab

Squab are young pigeons from three to four weeks old. They usually have a mass of less than 450 g (1 lb.). The meat is very tender and light in colour. Squabs are quite expensive and are usually roasted, although they can also be broiled or sautéed when split.

Cornish Game Hen

Cornish game hens have meat which is similar in appearance to that of chickens. They have only white meat, which is tender. They usually have a mass of less than 450

g (1 lb.). Cornish game hens are heavy breasted and may be prepared in the same way as squab.

Duckling

Ducklings are ducks under one year in age. They have a mass of between 1.8 kg and 2.7 kg (4 to 6 lb.). Ducklings have only dark, tender meat and a higher proportion of fat and bone than chickens.

Geese

Geese are usually under one year old and have a mass of between 4 and 5.4 kg (9 to 12 lb.). Geese have dark meat which is fatter than that of other birds. Geese are best roasted.

STORAGE OF POULTRY

perish—spoil

Poultry will **perish** very quickly. Fresh poultry should be refrigerated as soon as it is received. Remove the giblets from the neck or body cavity and store separately, as these will spoil more rapidly. If possible, fresh poultry should be packed in crushed ice and placed in the coldest part of the refrigerator. To minimize possible spoilage, it is a good practice to purchase fresh poultry the day before it is to be used. Frozen poultry should be kept frozen until a day or two before using. Frozen poultry should be thawed in the refrigerator or in cold running water.

COOKING METHODS FOR POULTRY

succulent—juicy

Generally, cooking methods for poultry are the same as those used for other meats. Old or tough birds are cooked by moist heat methods, while younger birds are more **succulent** when cooked by dry heat methods. However, regardless of the method of cooking, poultry should always be cooked well done. Larger birds should be cooked more slowly to reduce shrinkage and retain moisture. Smaller birds should be cooked more rapidly (190°–200°C or 375°–400°F) to prevent them from drying out while cooking. If stuffing or dressing is to be served with the bird, it is the practice in the commercial kitchen to stuff smaller birds but to make the dressing for larger birds separately. This saves time and makes serving easier.

RECIPES

Roasted and Baked Poultry

Roast Chicken

Approximate yield: 20 portions

10		roasting chickens approximately 1.4 kg (3 lb.) each
225 g	(8 oz.)	onions, cut in small dice ⎫
180 g	(6 oz.)	celery, cut in small dice ⎬ mirepoix
120 g	(4 oz.)	carrots, cut in small dice ⎭
225 g	(8 oz.)	shortening, melted
		salt to taste
		pepper to taste
225 g	(8 oz.)	flour
3 L	(3 qt.)	chicken stock, hot

Method

1. Season the inside of each bird with salt and pepper.
2. Spread the mirepoix in the bottom of a roasting pan.
3. Coat and rub the surface of each bird with melted shortening and place the birds in the roasting pan with the breasts up.
4. Roast the birds in a 190°C (375°F) oven until done (approximately 1 h). Turn the birds from side to side occasionally during the roasting period for more even roasting and browning.
5. Remove the chickens from the roasting pan and keep them warm.
6. Place the roasting pan on the range and cook the remaining fat to reduce the excess moisture in it.
7. Blend in the flour to make a roux and cook over low heat for about 5 min.
8. Add the hot chicken stock to the roux and blend well.
9. Simmer the gravy for about 15 min.
10. Strain the gravy and adjust the seasonings.

Roast turkey with wild rice stuffing (Courtesy of the Ontario Ministry of Agriculture and Food)

Roast Turkey
Approximate yield: 35 portions

11 kg	(24 lb.)	turkey
225 g	(8 oz.)	onions, cut in small dice ⎫
180 g	(6 oz.)	celery, cut in small dice ⎬ mirepoix
120 g	(4 oz.)	carrots, cut in small dice ⎭
90 mL	(3 oz.)	oil or melted shortening
		salt to taste
		pepper to taste
180 g	(6 oz.)	flour
3 L	(3 qt.)	chicken stock, hot

Method
1. Season the inside of the turkey with salt and pepper.
2. Rub the skin of the turkey with oil or melted shortening.
3. Place the turkey on its side in a roasting pan.
4. Roast in the oven at 180°C (350°F) for 1.5 h.
5. Turn the turkey onto its opposite side and roast for an additional 1.5 h.
6. Turn the turkey until the breast side is up, add the mirepoix, and continue cooking until done (approximately 1 h).

7. Remove the turkey from the roast pan to a warm place.
8. Prepare the gravy as described in the roast chicken recipe on page 123.

Roast Duckling à l'Orange   Yield: 20 portions

5		ducklings, 2.2–2.7 kg (5–6 lb.) each
		salt to taste
		pepper to taste
3		oranges
2		lemons
120 g	(4 oz.)	sugar
120 mL	(4 oz.)	red wine vinegar
225 mL	(8 oz.)	orange juice
2 L	(2 qt.)	brown sauce, hot

Method

1. Season the insides of the ducks with salt and pepper.
2. **Truss** the ducks and place them on racks in a roasting pan, breast side up.

   truss—to bind the wings of a bird before cooking

3. Roast the ducks in a 200°C (400°F) oven for 1.5 to 2 h, or until they are done. Turn the ducks periodically during cooking for even browning.
4. Peel the **zest** from the oranges and lemons.
5. Cut the zest in fine julienne strips and blanch it in boiling water for 5 min. Drain the zest and set it aside.

   zest—piece of orange or lemon peel used to give flavour

6. Squeeze the juice from the zested oranges and lemons. Combine the juices and set aside.
7. Place the sugar in a sauce pan and cook over low heat until the sugar has **caramelized**.

   caramelized—converted into burnt sugar

8. Add the vinegar, the combined fruit juices and the 225 mL (8 oz.) of orange juice.
9. Cook this until it is reduced by half.
10. Combine the reduction with the brown sauce and hold over low heat.
11. When the ducks are cooked, remove them from the roast pan and keep them warm.
12. Pour the fat from the roast pan and deglaze the pan with a little water.
13. Strain the deglaze liquid into the sauce and simmer the sauce for 5 min.
14. Serve one-quarter duck per portion, sprinkled with a little of the blanched zest and covered with 60 mL (2 oz.) of sauce.

Note: Ducks are roasted at a higher temperature than other poultry to extract the excess fat and to crisp the skin.

Chicken Breasts Florentine
Yield: 20 portions

10		chicken breasts, halved, skinned and boned
120 g	(4 oz.)	butter or margarine, melted
2		lemons
		salt to taste
		pepper to taste
2 kg	(4½ lb.)	spinach, cooked
180 g	(6 oz.)	butter or margarine
2 mL	(½ tsp.)	nutmeg, ground
1.5 L	(1½ qt.)	mornay sauce, hot (Chapter 8)
225 g	(8 oz.)	Parmesan cheese, grated

Method

1. Brush the chicken breasts with melted butter and season with salt and pepper.
2. Place the chicken breasts in a roast pan and sprinkle with the juice of two lemons.
3. Bake in a 200°C (400°F) oven for 15 min, or until the breasts are tender but not browned. Remove from the oven and keep warm.
4. Toss the cooked spinach with one-half of the butter or margarine and the nutmeg.
5. Spread the spinach in the bottom of a baking pan and place the cooked chicken breasts on top of the spinach.
6. Pour the mornay sauce over the chicken and the spinach.
7. Sprinkle the Parmesan cheese on top and dot with the remaining butter or margarine.
8. Place under the broiler to brown the cheese.
9. Serve with rice or noodles.

Fried and Sautéed Poultry

Chicken Cacciatore
Yield: 20 portions

10		1 kg (2 lb.) chickens, cut in pieces
450 g	(1 lb.)	flour, seasoned with salt and pepper
570 mL	(1 pt.)	vegetable oil
450 g	(1 lb.)	green peppers, sliced

450 g	(1 lb.)	onions, finely diced
450 g	(1 lb.)	mushrooms, sliced
3		cloves of garlic, finely chopped
2.5 L	(2½ qt.)	tomatoes, canned and crushed, with the juice
225 mL	(8 oz.)	brown stock
5 mL	(1 tsp.)	oregano
5 mL	(1 tsp.)	basil
		salt to taste
		pepper to taste

Method

1. Coat the chicken pieces with the seasoned flour and shake off the excess.
2. Heat the oil in a sauté pan and sauté the chicken pieces until they are golden brown.
3. Remove the chicken and let the pieces drain well.
4. Pour the oil from the sauté pan into a sauce pan.
5. Add the green peppers, onions, mushrooms and garlic and sauté until they are tender. Do not brown.
6. Add the brown stock and simmer for 5 min.
7. Add the crushed tomatoes and the juice, oregano and basil. Season to taste with salt and pepper.
8. Simmer for 5 min, stirring constantly.
9. Place the sautéed chicken in a brazier and pour the sauce over the chicken.
10. Bake in a 180°C (350°F) oven for 45 min, or until the chicken is tender.
11. Serve one-half chicken per portion with 90 mL (3 oz.) of sauce.

Chicken Chasseur
Yield: 20 portions

10		chickens, 1 kg (2 lb.) each, cut in pieces
		salt
		pepper
225 mL	(8 oz.)	vegetable oil
120 g	(4 oz.)	onions, finely diced
3		garlic cloves, finely chopped
900 g	(2 lb.)	mushrooms, sliced
360 mL	(12 oz.)	white stock
1.5 L	(1½ qt.)	tomatoes, canned
360 mL	(12 oz.)	demi-glace, hot

Method

1. Season the chicken pieces with salt and pepper.
2. Heat the oil in a sauté pan and brown the chicken pieces on all sides.
3. Remove the chicken pieces and drain well.
4. Pour off half of the oil in the sauté pan.
5. Add the onions, garlic and mushrooms and sauté until tender. Do not brown.
6. Add the white stock, tomatoes and demi-glace and bring to a boil.
7. Reduce to simmer and add the chicken pieces.
8. Cover and cook for 30 min, or until the chicken is tender.
9. Serve one-half chicken per portion with 90 mL (3 oz.) of sauce.

Broiled Poultry

Broiled Chicken Halves   Yield: 20 portions

10		broiling or frying chickens, 1 kg (2 lb.) each
120 mL	(4 oz.)	vegetable oil
225 g	(8 oz.)	butter, melted

Method

1. Clean the chickens and split them in half.
2. Rub the skin of the chickens with vegetable oil and season with salt.
3. Place the chickens, skin side up, on a preheated broiler and cook for several minutes until lightly browned.
4. Turn the chickens over with the skin side down and cook until the skin side is browned and well marked with grill marks.
5. Remove the chickens to a roast pan and bake at 180°C (350°F) until done (about 45 to 60 min).
6. Brush the chickens with melted butter before serving.

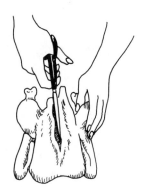

Boiled or Stewed Poultry

Chicken à la King   Approximate yield: 20 portions

2 kg	(4½ lb.)	cooked chicken meat with bones and skin removed, cut in 2.5 cm (1 in.) dice
450 g	(1 lb.)	mushrooms, sliced
450 g	(1 lb.)	butter or margarine

225 g	(8 oz.)	flour
1 L	(1 qt.)	chicken stock, hot
2 L	(2 qt.)	milk, hot
225 g	(8 oz.)	green peppers, small dice
120 g	(4 oz.)	pimientos, small dice
		salt

Method

1. Melt the butter in a sauce pan and sauté the mushrooms until they are soft.
2. Add the flour and cook slowly for 5 min to make a roux. Do not brown.
3. Add the hot chicken stock and stir until slightly thickened and smooth. Add the milk and blend well.
4. Cook the diced green peppers in boiling salted water for 5 min. Drain.
5. Add the green peppers and pimientos to the sauce.
6. Reheat the chicken meat in the stock it was cooked in and drain.
7. Combine the chicken with the sauce, mixing gently to prevent the meat from breaking up.
8. Serve 225 mL (8 oz.) portions with rice or in a patty shell.

Chicken Fricassee   Approximate yield: 20 portions

2 kg	(4½ lb.)	cooked chicken meat with the bones and skin removed
40		pearl onions, medium sized
40		mushroom caps, small
1		lemon
1.5 L	(1½ qt.)	velouté sauce, hot, made with chicken stock (See Chapter 8.)

Method

1. Cover the onions with cold water. Bring to a boil and simmer until they are tender but not soft. Drain well.
2. Cook the mushrooms in a small amount of boiling, salted water to which the juice of one lemon has been added. Drain well.
3. Heat the chicken meat in the stock it was cooked in. Drain well.
4. Combine the onions, mushrooms, chicken meat and velouté sauce.
5. Stir gently to mix the ingredients. Do not break up the chicken.
6. Serve with rice or buttered noodles.

Bread Stuffing

Approximate yield: 20 portions

1.4 kg	(3 lb.)	bread, preferably not fresh
675 g	(1 ½ lb.)	onions, finely diced
225 g	(8 oz.)	celery, finely diced
180 g	(6 oz.)	butter or margarine
8 mL	(1 ½ tsp.)	poultry seasoning
15 mL	(1 tbsp.)	thyme
15 mL	(1 tbsp.)	sage
15 mL	(1 tbsp.)	parsley, chopped
		salt to taste
		pepper to taste

Method

1. Remove the crusts from the bread and cut it into small cubes.
2. Soak the bread in cold water and drain well.
3. Sauté the onions and celery in the butter or margarine until they are tender.
4. Combine the onions, celery, bread and seasonings and mix lightly to blend.
5. Place in a greased baking pan and cover with greased paper.
6. Bake at 190°C (375°F) for 1 h.

Find the Answers to These Questions

1. What is (a) a capon? (b) a squab?
2. How should fresh poultry be stored?
3. Why should large birds be cooked more slowly than small birds?
4. Why are ducks roasted at higher temperatures than other poultry?
5. When is utility grade poultry a good buy?

CHAPTER 11
FISH

Watch for These Words

economical   criteria   shucked
dehydrating   entrails   discarded
assess   extract   moulted

How to Use These Words

1. Broiling or baking fish with a high fat content will help to __XXXX__ some of the fat.
2. Oysters sold with the shells removed are called __XXXX__ oysters.
3. Soft-shelled crabs, or crabs that have lost their shells, are crabs that have __XXXX__.
4. Packing fresh fish in ice prevents the fish from drying up or __XXXX__.
5. Fish is generally considered to be a cheap and __XXXX__ food source.
6. Before fish is cooked, the __XXXX__ are removed.
7. There are five __XXXX__ used to determine if fish is fresh.
8. Shellfish that do not have tightly closed shells should not be used; they should be __XXXX__.
9. When examining the fish, the student had difficulty trying to __XXXX__ its freshness.

Fish are high in nutritional value. They are excellent sources of vitamins, minerals and proteins. Fish are also easy to digest. Many fish are only available during certain times of the year. But despite this, fish is generally considered to be an **economical** food.

For commercial cookery purposes, fish can be classified as **fin fish** or **shellfish**. Fin fish are all the edible fresh and salt water fish which have fins. Shellfish are of two categories, **crustaceans** and **mollusks**. Crustaceans include shrimp, lobster, and crabs. Mollusks include oysters, clams, scallops and mussels.

economical—avoiding waste

131

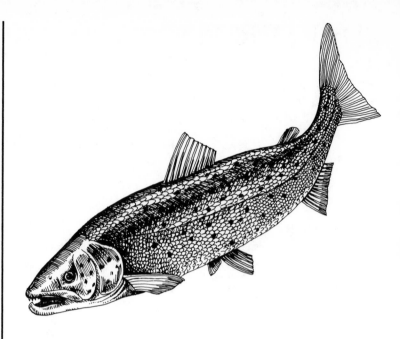

STORAGE OF FISH

Fresh fish is highly perishable. Therefore it must be kept refrigerated below a temperature of 4.5°C (40°F) at all times. Fresh fish should be refrigerated in crushed ice if possible. This will prevent the surface of the fish from **dehydrating** and spoiling. If crushed ice is not available, the fish should be wrapped in nonabsorbent paper and stored in the refrigerator. If possible, fish should be stored in a separate refrigerator. This will prevent fish odours from spreading to other refrigerated foods. Frozen fish should be kept frozen until it is to be used. Never refreeze thawed fish!

WHAT TO LOOK FOR WHEN PURCHASING FRESH FISH

To maintain high standards of quality, it is necessary to be able to **assess** the freshness of fish before accepting it in the kitchen. There are five **criteria** used to determine the freshness of fish:

1. The eyes should be clear and bright.
2. The gills should be bright red and not slimy to the touch.
3. The scales should adhere tightly to the skin and have a bright and shiny appearance.
4. The flesh should be firm with an **elasticity** which allows it to spring back when it is pressed.

dehydrating—drying out

assess—find out the amount of
criteria—standards

elasticity—springiness

5. The odour should be fresh, not objectionable or overly fishy.

HOW FISH ARE MARKETED

Fish may be purchased in various forms, depending on the requirements of the kitchen. Factors which influence the form in which fish is purchased are cost, convenience and availability of skilled labour in the kitchen. The more the fish is **processed** before purchasing, the more convenient it is to serve and the more it will cost.

Whole fish are those that are sold just as they were taken from the water, without any processing. Before they can be cooked, the scales and **entrails** must be removed along with the head, fins and tail.

Drawn fish are those that have the entrails removed before being sold. Scales, head, fins and tail remain. These must be removed in the kitchen before preparation.

Dressed fish have the entrails, scales, head, fins and tail removed before they are sold.

Steaks are cross-section slices of larger dressed fish. One steak is usually enough for an individual portion. The only bone present in steaks is a section of the backbone.

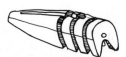

Fillets are the sides of the fish cut lengthwise from the backbone. There are two fillets on each fish and they are usually boneless.

Fish are also marketed in a variety of preserved forms. These include smoked fish (smoked cod, haddock, herring and salmon), pickled fish (pickled herring) and salted fish (salted cod and mackerel). Fish preserved in these ways is usually made into canapés and hors-d'oeuvres or used in buffets.

dressed fish

fillets

COOKING METHODS

Most fish do not require a lot of cooking time. Since fish have no connective tissue, too much heat and overcooking must be avoided. It would destroy the nutrients, taste and appearance of the fish.

Not all fish are suitable for every method of cooking. Some fish have a higher fat content than others. Often this determines the cooking method. Fish with a high fat content are more suited to broiling or baking. Either method will help to **extract** excess fat. Lean fish are not particularly well suited to dry heat methods of cooking, although such methods are sometimes used. The following chart lists a variety of common fish, indicating whether they are fat or lean and what cooking methods are appropriate for them.

extract—take out

Cooking Methods for Fish

Variety of Fish	Composition	Cooking Methods
bluefish	lean	Sauté, poach, deep fry
cod	lean	Broil, bake, boil, steam
sole	lean	Sauté, bake, poach, deep fry, steam
haddock	lean	Broil, bake, boil, steam, poach, deep fry
halibut	lean	Broil, bake, boil, steam, deep fry
mackerel	fat	Broil, bake
perch	lean	Pan fry, broil
red snapper	lean	Bake, broil
sea bass	lean	Bake, broil
swordfish	lean	Broil, bake, deep fry
smelt	lean	Pan fry, deep fry
trout	fat	Pan fry, broil, bake
whitefish	fat	Broil, bake
pickerel	lean	Pan fry, broil
salmon	fat	Broil, bake, poach, steam

SHELLFISH

Shellfish are nutritious, low in fat and rich in protein. They are highly perishable, especially if **shucked**. Crustaceans, such as shrimp and lobster, can be frozen. However, this does toughen them somewhat. Mollusks, such as

shucked—having had the shell removed

oysters, clams and scallops, should have tightly closed shells. Shells that will not close indicate that the animal is dead and should be **discarded**.

discarded—thrown away

Crustaceans

The **edible** portion of a **shrimp** is the fresh, frozen or cooked tail section. The head and body are generally removed before the shrimp are marketed. If the shell is not removed, the shrimp are sold according to size. But shrimp are also sold peeled and deveined. This means that the shell and the intestinal tract have been removed. Shrimp can also be purchased breaded and ready for deep frying or as salad shrimp. These are small or broken shrimp with the shells removed.

edible—able to be eaten

Shrimp require very little cooking. Great care must be taken not to overcook them or they become tough and rubbery. Cooking methods for shrimp include boiling, sautéing and deep frying. Large shrimp may be stuffed and baked.

Lobsters are available in a variety of forms. They may be purchased live or as cooked meat, either fresh or frozen. In addition, frozen lobster tails are marketed in a

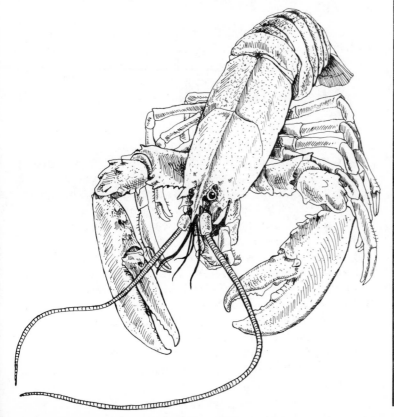

variety of sizes. Live lobsters are usually from the cold waters of the North Atlantic Ocean. These lobsters have large claws which contain succulent meat.

Lobsters must be alive when they are cooked. If they are dead before they are cooked, the meat will flake and fall apart after cooking. It is best to store live lobsters covered with seaweed and under refrigeration. Cooking methods for lobster include boiling, broiling, steaming and baking.

Frozen lobster tails usually come from warm-water lobsters, which have no claws. Most of their meat comes from the tail. Lobster tails are usually broiled or baked.

Most **crab** is sold cooked and frozen. Small live crabs are usually of the soft-shelled varieties. These are crabs that have **moulted** and have not yet grown new shells. Soft-shelled crabs must be cleaned before cooking. They are usually served sautéed or deep fried. Alaskan king crabs are large crabs which have long, meat-filled legs. Their body meat is usually canned. Leg meat can be purchased frozen or cooked in the shell. Alaskan king crab legs are usually served broiled or baked.

moulted—shed their shells

Mollusks

Oysters may be purchased live in the shell or shucked, and also fresh or frozen. Fresh oysters are plump and surrounded by a clear, gelatinous liquid. Oysters in the shell may be served as appetizers raw on the half-shell, baked or stuffed and baked. Shucked oysters are used for chowder, stew and deep frying.

Clams are available in several varieties and sizes. Small, soft-shelled clams are cooked by steaming. They are then served in the shell with the broth they were cooked in and melted butter. Little neck and cherrystone clams are served raw on the half-shell as appetizers. The larger clams are not tender. Usually they are used for clam chowder and for deep frying. Shucked clams are available primarily for use in chowder or for deep frying.

Scallops may be sea scallops or bay scallops. The sea scallops are larger in size and have a coarse texture. Bay scallops are smaller in size and have a more delicate flavour and a finer texture. The edible portion of the scallop is the muscle which opens and closes the scallop shell. Scallops are sold already shucked and they may be fresh or frozen. Sometimes various seafood dishes are served in scallop shells. Scallops may be broiled, sautéed, deep fried and poached.

Mussels are available fresh in the shell and shucked. They have coral-coloured flesh with an **elongated** blue-black shell. Mussels must be soaked in fresh water to remove any sand from inside their shells. In addition, they have a tuft of hairs which must be removed with a knife. Mussels may be served steamed in the shell accompanied by their broth and melted butter, or baked in the half-shell.

elongated—long and narrow

RECIPES

Deep-Fried Sole   Yield: 20 portions

Most lean fish, such as sole, bluefish, cod and halibut, are best suited for deep frying. Fish must be breaded or dipped in batter before deep frying to provide a crisp, golden-brown coating.

20		sole fillets, 150 g (5 oz.) each
450 g	(1 lb.)	flour
6		eggs
1 L	(1 qt.)	milk
675 mL	(1 1/4 pt.)	bread crumbs
		salt and pepper to taste

Method

1. Place the flour in a bake pan and season with salt and pepper.
2. Prepare an egg wash by adding the milk to the lightly beaten eggs.
3. Place the bread crumbs in a bake pan.
4. Add the sole fillets to the seasoned flour and coat them thoroughly. Shake off any excess flour.
5. Place each floured sole fillet in the egg wash and allow excess egg wash to run off the fillets.
6. Place each sole fillet in the pan of bread crumbs. Thoroughly coat the fillets with the bread crumbs. Lightly shake off any excess bread crumbs.
7. Place the breaded fillets in a fry basket a few at a time. Deep fry at 180°C (350°F) until they are golden-brown and cooked.
8. Remove the fish from the fryer and let them drain well.
9. Serve garnished with lemon and tartar sauce.

Deep-Fried Halibut   Yield: 20 portions

660 g	(1 lb. 6 oz.)	flour	} batter
30 g	(1 oz.)	yeast	
750 mL	(3 cups)	water	
		salt to taste	
20		halibut pieces, 150 g (5 oz.) each	
450 g	(1 lb.)	flour seasoned with salt and pepper	

Method

1. Prepare the batter by sifting flour and salt into a bowl.
2. Dissolve the yeast in a little of the water.
3. Make a well in the flour and add the yeast and the water.
4. Gradually mix the flour, the water and the yeast and beat to a smooth mixture.
5. Let the batter stand for 1 h before using.
6. Coat the halibut pieces with seasoned flour and shake off the excess.
7. Dip the floured halibut into the batter and let the excess batter run off.
8. Gently lower the batter-coated halibut into the deep fryer and fry at a temperature of 180°C (350°F) until golden-brown and cooked.
9. Drain well before serving.

trout—fish of the salmon family, found chiefly in fresh water. The most common in N. America are the brown trout, rainbow trout, brook trout and lake trout.

Trout Meunière   Yield: 20 portions

20		small trout, 225 g (8 oz.) each, dressed and cleaned
570 mL	(1 pt.)	milk
900 g	(2 lb.)	flour
225 g	(8 oz.)	butter
300 mL	(10 oz.)	vegetable oil
60 g	(2 oz.)	parsley, chopped
90 mL	(3 oz.)	lemon juice
450 g	(1 lb.)	butter

Method

1. Dip the **trout** in lightly seasoned milk.
2. Coat each trout with flour and shake off any excess.
3. Heat the butter and oil in a large frying pan.

4. Sauté the trout for about 6 min on each side until they are nicely browned.
5. Remove the trout to a lightly oiled pan and keep them warm in the oven.
6. Heat the 450 g (1 lb.) of butter in a frying pan until lightly browned. Add the lemon juice.
7. Sprinkle chopped parsley over the trout and pour the browned butter over it.
8. Serve immediately.

Broiled Salmon Steak   Yield: 20 portions

20		salmon steaks, 180 g (6 oz.) each
225 mL	(8 oz.)	vegetable oil
60 g	(2 oz.)	paprika
		salt and pepper to taste

salmon—silver-scaled, pink-fleshed fish that live in salt water and spawn in fresh water

Method

1. Dip the **salmon** steaks in the oil.
2. Season the steaks with salt and pepper. Sprinkle paprika on both sides.
3. Place the salmon steaks on a hot broiler rack and broil 15 cm (6 in.) from the heat for about 5 min on each side.
4. Serve with chopped, fresh parsley and melted butter or an appropriate sauce, for example caper or dill sauce.

Stuffed Fillet of Flounder   Yield: 20 portions

20		flounder fillets, 150–180 g (5–6 oz.) each
1.6 kg	(3½ lb.)	crabmeat
300 g	(10 oz.)	celery, finely diced
300 g	(10 oz.)	onions, finely diced
150 g	(5 oz.)	green peppers, finely diced
300 g	(10 oz.)	butter
90 g	(3 oz.)	flour
1 L	(1 qt.)	milk, hot
45 mL	(3 tbsp.)	Worcestershire sauce
1 mL	(¼ tsp.)	tabasco sauce
225 mL	(8 oz.)	bread crumbs
3		egg yolks
		salt and pepper to taste

flounder—any flatfish other than sole

Method

1. Melt the butter in a sauce pan.
2. Add the celery, onions and green peppers and sauté until they are just tender.
3. Add the flour to make a roux and cook for a few minutes.
4. Add the hot milk and stir with a whisk until the mixture thickens.
5. Add the crabmeat, Worcestershire sauce, and tabasco sauce.
6. Mix well, cook for a few minutes and remove from the heat.
7. Stir in the bread crumbs and egg yolks. Season with salt and pepper.
8. When the mixture has cooled slightly, place a portion on each fillet. Roll up the fillet and fasten it with a toothpick.
9. Place the stuffed fillets in a lightly oiled baking pan and bake at 180°C (350°F) for about 30 min.
10. Remove from the oven and serve with mornay sauce or cardinal sauce.

Poached Salmon   Yield: 20 portions

20		salmon steaks, 150–180 g (5–6 oz.) each
2 L	(2 qt.)	court bouillon, hot (See Chapter 7.)
120 g	(4 oz.)	butter or margarine

Method

1. Prepare the court bouillon.
2. Use the butter or margarine to lightly grease a baking pan.
3. Place the salmon steaks in the baking pan and barely cover with hot court bouillon.
4. Gently poach the salmon on top of the range or in the oven at a temperature of 180°C (350°F) for about 20 min.
5. Carefully remove the salmon steaks and serve them with a suitable sauce.

Note: Whole fish and fillets of fish may be prepared in the same manner.

Fillets of Sole Bonne Femme   Yield: 20 portions

20	pieces of fillets of sole, 150–180 g (5–6 oz.) each

120 g	(4 oz.)	butter or margarine
450 g	(1 lb.)	mushrooms, sliced
60 g	(2 oz.)	green onions, chopped
30 g	(1 oz.)	parsley, chopped
1 L	(1 qt.)	court bouillon, hot
90 g	(3 oz.)	butter
120 g	(4 oz.)	flour
225 mL	(8 oz.)	cream, 35% (whipping cream)
		salt and pepper to taste

Method

1. Prepare the court bouillon (see Chapter 7) and simmer to reduce it by one-third. Strain.
2. Use butter or margarine to lightly grease a baking pan.
3. Place the fillets of sole in the greased baking pan.
4. Add the sliced mushrooms, chopped green onions, chopped parsley and the reduced and strained court bouillon.
5. Bring the ingredients in the baking pan to a boil on top of the range.
6. Place the baking pan in a 180°C (350°F) oven and poach the fillets of sole until done (5–7 min).
7. Remove the baking pan from the oven.
8. Strain off the liquid from the pan and reserve the liquid and the vegetables separately.
9. Keep the fillets of sole warm.
10. Prepare a roux from the butter and flour. Cook for 5 min.
11. Slowly add the strained liquid to the roux and whisk until the sauce is slightly thickened.
12. Add the vegetables to the sauce.
13. Season the sauce to taste with salt and pepper and add the cream.
14. Continue cooking until the sauce is hot. Do not boil.
15. Serve one fillet of sole covered with sauce per portion.

Shrimp Creole   Approximate yield: 20 portions

| 2.7 kg | (6 lb.) | cooked shrimp |
| 2 L | (2 qt.) | Creole sauce (See Chapter 8.) |

Method

1. Boil the shrimp, being careful not to overcook them.
2. Remove the shells and **devein** the shrimp with the point of a sharp knife.

devein—remove the intestinal tract

3. Bring the Creole sauce to a simmer and add the cooked shrimp.
4. Blend the shrimp into the sauce by gently mixing with a spoon and bring the mixture back to a simmer.
5. Serve over steamed or baked rice.

Mussels in Cream

Approximate yield: 20 portions

10 L	(10 qt.)	mussels
120 g	(4 oz.)	butter
450 g	(1 lb.)	carrots, sliced
		parsley
		thyme
		chervil } bouquet garni
		tarragon
900 g	(2 lb.)	mushrooms, chopped
60 g	(2 oz.)	butter
180 g	(6 oz.)	flour
1 L	(1 qt.)	heavy cream
		lemon juice from half a lemon
120 g	(4 oz.)	parsley, chopped
		salt and pepper to taste

Method

1. Scrub the mussels with a stiff brush and wash them several times in cold water. Scrape off the beards, or tufts of hair, and discard any mussels with open shells.
2. Melt the 120 g (4 oz.) of butter in a large pot. Add the sliced carrots and the bouquet garni.
3. Cook the mixture slowly for about 20 min, or until the carrots are tender.
4. Add the mussels. Cover the pot tightly and cook over high heat for 4 to 5 min, or until the shells of the mussels open.
5. Discard one shell from each mussel and keep the mussels warm in a covered pan.
6. Cook the chopped mushrooms in the 60 g (2 oz.) of butter until they are tender.
7. Stir in the flour and cook, while stirring, for a few minutes. Do not allow the mixture to brown.
8. Strain the mussel broth through cheesecloth and gradually add it to the mushroom and flour mixture.
9. Cook for 5 min, stirring constantly.

10. Season to taste with salt and pepper and add the heavy cream and lemon juice.
11. Heat the sauce for a few minutes but do not allow it to boil.
12. Arrange the mussels on heated platters and serve them coated with the sauce. Sprinkle chopped parsley over the mussels.

Broiled Lobster Tails   Yield: 1 portion

2 lobster tails, 120 g (4 oz.) each
vegetable oil
paprika
salt and pepper to taste
melted butter
lemon slices

Method

1. Hold the lobster tail, shell side up, firmly with a towel.
2. Split the shell in half lengthwise with a French knife.
3. Spread the split shell slightly and bring the tail meat carefully outside to rest on the shell. The meat should still be attached to the shell at the body end of the tail.
4. Place the lobster tails in a bake pan, flesh side up. Coat the lobster meat with vegetable oil.
5. Season with salt and pepper and sprinkle on some paprika.
6. Broil under a low flame until the meat browns slightly and the shell turns red.
7. Remove the lobster tails from the broiler and finish cooking them in the oven at 180°C (350°F). A total cooking time of 15 to 20 min is usually enough.
8. Serve the lobster tails with melted butter and lemon.

Find the Answers to These Questions

1. How are fish classified?
2. Describe the storage procedure for fresh fish.
3. What are the five criteria used to determine if fish is fresh?
4. Describe a fish steak.
5. What are the two categories of shellfish?
6. Why must lobsters be alive before they are cooked?
7. What is a soft-shelled crab?
8. Why must mussels be soaked in fresh water?

CHAPTER 12
VEGETABLES

Watch for These Words

hasty   reaction   detected
blanched   sulphur   soundness
chlorophyll   minimized
intensify   rotated

How to Use These Words

1. When green vegetables are cooked in an alkaline solution, it tends to __XXXX__ their colour.
2. The spoiled vegetables were __XXXX__ by the cook while he was looking for potatoes.
3. Frozen vegetables are __XXXX__ before they are frozen.
4. Red cabbage should be cooked uncovered to allow the __XXXX__ to escape.
5. Because the cook had almost forgotten to cook vegetables for lunch, their preparation was __XXXX__.
6. The cook doubted the __XXXX__ of the green beans because the can was swollen.
7. The risk of the peeled potatoes becoming discoloured was __XXXX__ because they were covered with cold water.
8. Stocks of canned vegetables must be __XXXX__ on a regular basis to minimize spoilage.
9. The __XXXX__ of red vegetables with acidic water during cooking improves their red colour.
10. __XXXX__ is the substance from which green vegetables get their colour.

Today most people are very aware of nutritional values. Therefore it is important for you to know about basic nutrition and the role that effective vegetable cookery plays in good nutrition. Vegetables are an important part of a meal, yet their preparation is often **hasty** or careless.

hasty—thoughtless or hurried

145

Shopping for fresh vegetables (Courtesy of the Ontario Ministry of Industry and Tourism)

alkalies—substances that neutralize acids

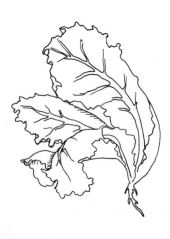

Vegetables provide the body with valuable vitamins and minerals. They also help to maintain the body's reserves of **alkalies**. The extent to which the nutritional benefits of vegetables, as well as their flavour and colour, are preserved depends largely on proper cooking methods.

In Canada, vegetables are graded according to federal government regulations before they can be exported or shipped between provinces. The federal grade designations are Canada No. 1 and Canada No. 2. Canada No. 1 grade rates higher in shape, cleanliness, size, and freedom from blemishes and disease.

Vegetables are available in four forms:
    fresh
    frozen
    canned
    dried

Fresh vegetables should be washed well before cooking. Leaf vegetables should be washed several times in cold water to make sure that dirt and sand are removed from between the leaves. Be sure to remove the leaf greens from the water rather than the water from the leaf greens. This ensures that the dirt and sand will settle to the bottom of the sink and not back into the leaf vegetables. Vegetables that are to be cooked in their skins should be well scrubbed. Those vegetables that are to be peeled should be carefully pared to remove a thin layer of skin. This reduces waste and also helps to retain the nutrients in the vegetable, since the nutrients are right below the skin. Clean peelings and trimmings from vegetables may be used in making stock.

To cook fresh vegetables, first heat enough water to cover the vegetables. Once it has been brought to the boil, pour it over the vegetables. Add a small amount of salt, then bring the water back to the boil as quickly as possible. The vegetables should be cooked until they are slightly tender with some crispness left. They should then be taken off the heat, cooled with cold running water and drained well. These cooked vegetables are then reheated and seasoned with salt, pepper and sometimes sugar as they are needed for service.

Frozen vegetables are cooked in the same way as fresh vegetables. Cooking time is less for frozen vegetables, since they are **blanched** before they are frozen. Most frozen vegetables can be cooked from their frozen state. Exceptions to this are frozen leaf greens such as spinach, which should be completely thawed. This allows the leaves to be separated for more uniform cooking. Always remember that frozen vegetables should never be re-frozen once they are thawed.

Canned vegetables are fully cooked before they are put in the can. They require only reheating and seasoning before serving. Always reheat canned vegetables in their own liquid and in small quantities as needed. Do not over-cook canned vegetables. If canned vegetables are not prepared according to the above rules, much of their nutritional value will be lost.

Dried vegetables are legumes such as peas, lentils and beans. They have all the water in them removed. They are mostly used in soup making. Dried legumes should be soaked at room temperature for five or six hours to allow them to replace their lost water. Soaking is not required for lentils or split peas. Legumes should be simmered, never boiled, during cooking. Boiling toughens them.

VEGETABLE COLOURS

Vegetables are classified according to their colour. The colours of vegetables are:
    green
    red
    yellow
    white

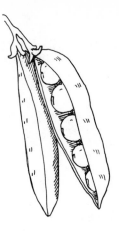

blanched—immersed briefly in boiling water and then quickly cooled

chlorophyll—the substance which produces green colour in plants

intensify—heighten or increase

reaction—response

sulphur—a pale yellow, nonmetallic chemical element

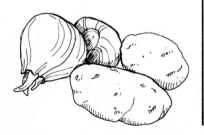

Green Vegetables

Green vegetables derive their natural colour from a substance called **chlorophyll**. Chlorophyll is affected by alkalies and acids in the presence of heat. Most green vegetables contain a high percentage of acid. The acid can destroy the chlorophyll. Therefore green vegetables should be cooked uncovered to allow the acid to escape in the steam. Use a small amount of boiling, salted water and cook the vegetables in as short a time as possible. In an alkaline solution, the green colour in vegetables becomes extremely bright. Baking soda is an alkali which will **intensify** the colour of green vegetables. However, the use of baking soda is **not** recommended because it destroys the vitamin content and the flavour of vegetables and makes them mushy as well.

Red Vegetables

When heat is applied to red vegetables, the **reaction** is exactly opposite to that which occurs in the cooking of green vegetables. Alkaline water gives red vegetables a bluish grey colour, while acidic water improves their red colour. Thus red vegetables should be cooked covered so that they may benefit from their own acids. The exception to this rule is red cabbage, which contains **sulphur**. Sulphur gives off a strong, undesirable odour. Red cabbage should be cooked uncovered to allow the sulphur content to escape in the steam.

Yellow Vegetables

Yellow vegetables are not affected by any colour change unless they are overcooked. Overcooking will make them dull and unappetizing in appearance. Most yellow vegetables should be cooked in a small amount of salted water and covered so that nutrients do not escape with the steam.

White Vegetables

White vegetables become dull and grey in appearance when they are overcooked. To prevent this, cook these vegetables in just enough water to cover them. Cook them without a lid until they are just barely tender.

VEGETABLE STORAGE

Fresh vegetables such as onions and potatoes should be stored in a cool, dry location. All other fresh vegetables must be refrigerated to preserve their flavour and appearance. Peeled or cut vegetables must be stored in the refrigerator and their exposure to air **minimized** by sealing them in plastic bags, covering them with water or treating them with an oxidizing agent to prevent discolouration.

All frozen vegetables should be stored at a temperature between –18°C (0°F) and –12°C (10°F). Temperature ranges above these may reduce storage life and the quality of the vegetables. Once frozen vegetables have been thawed, under no circumstances must they be refrozen.

Canned vegetables should be stored in a cool, dry location where they will not be exposed to sunlight. Stocks of canned vegetables should be properly **rotated**. When a new shipment arrives, move the old stock forward and store the new stock behind the older stock. You can **detect** the spoilage of canned vegetables by looking for swollen or distorted cans or a spurting of contents when the can is opened. Remember, don't take chances with canned food. If there is any doubt about the **soundness** of the contents of a can, throw it out!

Dried vegetables should be stored in a cool, dry place in covered bins or bags.

minimized—lessened or reduced

rotated—revolved

detect—recognize or discover

soundness—not injured, diseased or rotten

RULES FOR THE PROPER COOKING OF VEGETABLES

Do:

1. use just enough water to cover the vegetables.
2. use only salted, boiling water.
3. cook the vegetables in quantities that are as small as possible.
4. cook the vegetables until they are just tender.
5. cook the vegetables as close to the time you serve them as possible.
6. cool the cooked vegetables in cold running water immediately if they are not to be served right away.
7. save the liquid the vegetables were cooked in. It can be used for reheating the vegetables or for soups and sauces.
8. season the vegetables to taste just before serving.
9. cut the vegetables in uniform size pieces for even cooking.

Do not:

1. let vegetables soak before cooking, with the exception of some dried legumes.

2. use too much water. This results in the loss of nutrients and flavour.
3. overcook the vegetables.
4. let the cooked vegetables stand in hot water after cooking. They will continue to cook.
5. add baking soda to green vegetables. This will make the vegetables mushy and will destroy the natural vitamins.
6. cook vegetables in large quantities. Appearance, flavour and nutritional value will all suffer.
7. thaw frozen vegetables too far in advance of cooking. Nutritional value may be lost and the danger of spoilage is increased.

A vegetable dish (Courtesy of the Ontario Ministry of Agriculture and Food)

RECIPES

Buttered Asparagus   Approximate yield: 20 portions

3.6 kg	(8 lb.)	fresh asparagus spears
10 mL	(2 tsp.)	salt
		boiling water to cover
225 g	(8 oz.)	melted butter

Method

1. Cut the tough ends off the asparagus.
2. Lightly peel the stalks with a potato peeler.

3. Tie the spears into bundles, using ten spears for each bundle.
4. Stand the bundles of asparagus in a sauce pan.
5. Pour the boiling water over the asparagus until it comes to 1.25 cm (½ in.) below the tips.
6. Add the salt and simmer uncovered until the stalks are tender.
7. Drain carefully and serve with melted butter.

Buttered Green Beans   Approximate yield: 20 portions

1.8 kg	(4 lb.)	frozen green beans
120 g	(4 oz.)	butter
		salted, boiling water to cover
		salt and pepper to taste

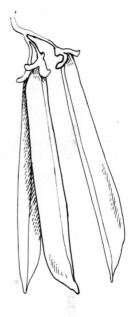

Method

1. Place the green beans in a sauce pan.
2. Add the boiling, salted water to cover the green beans.
3. When the water is boiling again, reduce the heat and cook for 8 to 10 min, or until the beans are tender.
4. Drain, add the butter and season to taste with salt and pepper.

Variation

For **green beans amandine**, cook the beans until they are just underdone. Sauté sliced almonds in butter until they are lightly browned. Add the green beans to the almonds and toss to blend the flavours.

Note: Fresh green beans may be substituted in the recipes.

Buttered Beets   Approximate yield: 20 portions

2.7 kg	(6 lb.)	fresh beets
		salted water to cover
120 g	(4 oz.)	butter
		salt and pepper to taste

Method

1. Trim the stems of the beets and leave the roots on.
2. Wash the beets thoroughly and place them in a sauce pan with salted water to cover.

3. Bring the beets to a boil, reduce the heat and simmer for 45 to 50 min, or until they are tender.
4. Strain the cooked beets and cool them in cold running water.
5. Peel the cooled beets and trim off the stems and roots.
6. Slice or dice the beets in uniform sizes.
7. Reheat the beets in the butter and season with salt and pepper to taste.

Buttered Broccoli
Approximate yield: 20 portions

3.2 kg	(7 lb.)	fresh broccoli
225 g	(8 oz.)	butter
		boiling, salted water to cover

Method

1. Remove the outer leaves and tough stem ends from the broccoli.
2. Wash the broccoli carefully in cold, salted water.
3. If the broccoli has tough or woody stems, peel the stems with a vegetable peeler and split them in half part way up.
4. Place the broccoli in a baking pan and cover it with boiling, salted water.
5. Cover the baking pan with a clean, wet towel for uniform cooking of the broccoli.
6. Simmer on top of the range for 15 to 20 min, or until the stems are tender. Do not overcook or the blossoms will fall apart.
7. Drain well and serve each portion with melted butter.

Variations

For **broccoli hollandaise**, mask each portion of broccoli with hollandaise sauce (Chapter 8) before serving. Use approximately 1 L (1 qt.) of sauce for 20 portions. For **broccoli with cheese sauce**, cover each portion with cheese sauce (Chapter 8) before serving. Use approximately 1 L (1 qt.) of sauce for 20 portions.

Note: Frozen broccoli may be substituted for fresh broccoli. Use 1.8 kg (4 lb.) frozen broccoli for 3.2 kg (7 lb.) fresh broccoli.

Buttered Brussels Sprouts Approximate yield: 20 portions

2.2 kg	(5 lb.)	fresh Brussels sprouts
		boiling, salted water to cover
120 g	(4 oz.)	butter
		salt and pepper to taste

Method

1. Remove any wilted and discoloured leaves from the Brussels sprouts. Trim the stems.
2. Soak the sprouts in cold, salted water for about 30 min.
3. Drain the Brussels sprouts and place them in a sauce pan.
4. Add the boiling, salted water to cover.
5. Simmer for 10 to 15 min, or until the Brussels sprouts are tender.
6. Drain well, add the butter and season with salt and pepper to taste before serving.

Variation

For **creamed Brussels sprouts**, add 1.5 L (1 ½ qt.) of cream sauce (Chapter 8) to the cooked Brussels sprouts before serving.

Buttered Cabbage   Approximate yield: 20 portions

3.6 kg	(8 lb.)	cabbage
120 g	(4 oz.)	butter
		boiling, salted water to cover
		salt and pepper to taste

Method

1. Remove the outer leaves from the cabbage.
2. Trim and wash the cabbage.
3. Cut the heads of cabbage into 20 wedges. Do not remove the core.
4. Place the wedges in a baking pan.
5. Add boiling, salted water to cover.
6. Simmer uncovered on top of the range until the cabbage is tender. Do not overcook.
7. Drain. Add the butter and season with salt and pepper before serving.

Braised Red Cabbage

Approximate yield: 20 portions

3.6 kg	(8 lb.)	red cabbage, trimmed and coarsely chopped
225 g	(8 oz.)	shortening
360 g	(12 oz.)	onions, finely diced
450 g	(1 lb.)	apples, peeled, cored and diced
750 mL	(3 cups)	boiling, salted water
90 g	(3 oz.)	sugar
90 mL	(3 oz.)	cider vinegar
		salt and pepper to taste

Method

1. Sauté the onions with the shortening in a sauce pan until they are partially cooked.
2. Add the cabbage, apples, sugar and boiling, salted water.
3. Simmer uncovered for 15 to 20 min, or until the cabbage is almost tender.
4. Add the vinegar, salt and pepper and cook for an additional 5 min.

Buttered Carrots

Approximate yield: 20 portions

2.2 kg	(5 lb.)	carrots
		boiling, salted water to cover
120 g	(4 oz.)	butter
		salt and pepper to taste

Method

1. Peel the carrots and slice them in uniformly thin slices.
2. Place the carrots in a sauce pan and add boiling, salted water to cover.
3. Simmer the carrots until they are tender.
4. Drain, add the butter and season to taste with salt and pepper before serving.

Variation

For **carrots Vichy**, add to the sliced carrots: 225 g (8 oz.) finely diced onions, 60 g (2 oz.) butter, 20 mL (4 tsp.) sugar. Cook as above and sprinkle chopped parsley on the cooked carrots.

Buttered Cauliflower

Approximate yield: 20 portions

2.7 kg	(6 lb.)	cauliflower, fresh or frozen
		boiling, salted water to cover
180 g	(6 oz.)	butter
		salt and pepper to taste

Method

1. Place the cauliflower in a sauce pan and add enough boiling, salted water to cover.
2. When the water returns to the boil, reduce the heat and simmer until the cauliflower is just tender.
3. Drain well and add the butter, salt and pepper before serving.

Cauliflower Polonaise

Approximate yield: 20 portions

2.7 kg	(6 lb.)	cauliflower, fresh or frozen
		boiling, salted water to cover
		pepper to taste
180 g	(6 oz.)	butter
480 mL	(16 oz.)	fresh bread crumbs
2		hard-cooked eggs, chopped
60 g	(2 oz.)	parsley, chopped

Method

1. Cook the cauliflower as in the recipe above.
2. Drain the cooked cauliflower and place it in a buttered baking pan.
3. Season with pepper and cover the cauliflower with a clean, damp towel.
4. Place the butter in a sauce pan and brown lightly.
5. Add the bread crumbs and cook until they are golden brown.
6. Remove the bread crumbs from the heat and blend in the hard-cooked eggs and parsley.
7. Sprinkle each portion of cauliflower with the bread crumb mixture when serving.

Braised Celery

Approximate yield: 20 portions

2.7 kg	(6 lb.)	celery
120 g	(4 oz.)	butter
90 g	(3 oz.)	flour
1.5 L	(1½ qt.)	chicken stock, hot
		salt and pepper to taste

Method

1. Remove root ends and leaves from the celery.
2. Wash the celery thoroughly and trim if necessary.
3. Cut the celery in 2.5 cm (1 in.) pieces.
4. Sauté the celery in butter until it is almost tender.
5. Stir in the flour and cook for a few minutes while stirring to avoid scorching.
6. Add the hot stock gradually, while stirring, until the mixture is thickened and smooth.
7. Bring the mixture to a boil and transfer it to a buttered baking pan.
8. Cover with foil and bake at 180°C (350°F) for 20 to 30 min, or until the celery is tender and the liquid is reduced by one-third.
9. Season to taste with salt and pepper.

Corn on the Cob   Yield: 20 portions

20 ears of corn
    unsalted, boiling water to cover
    butter

Method

1. Remove the husks and corn silk from the ears of corn.
2. Place the corn in a large pot and add boiling water to cover. Cover the pot.
3. When the water returns to the boil, cook the corn for about 4 to 8 min.
4. Remove the pot from the heat and keep the corn in the cooking liquid until it is time to serve.
5. Serve each ear of corn with a generous amount of butter.

Note: Fresh, young corn requires a minimum amount of cooking time.

Older corn may benefit from the addition of a little sugar to the water.

Always cook corn as close to the serving time as possible.

Buttered Kernel Corn   Approximate yield: 20 portions

2.2 kg	(5 lb.)	whole kernel corn, frozen
		boiling, salted water to cover
120 g	(4 oz.)	butter
		salt and pepper to taste

Method

1. Place the corn kernels in a sauce pan and add boiling, salted water to cover.
2. When the water returns to the boil, reduce the heat and cook until the corn is tender, about 3 to 5 min. Do not overcook.
3. Drain the cooked corn and add the butter, salt and pepper before serving.

Variation

For **Mexican-style corn**, sauté finely chopped green pepper and **pimientos**. Add to the cooked corn and sauté together for a few minutes to blend the flavours.

pimiento—a sweet red pepper

Deep-Fried Eggplant   Approximate yield: 20 portions

1.8 kg	(4 lb.)	eggplant
450 g	(1 lb.)	flour, seasoned
1 L	(1 qt.)	egg wash (see page 111)
675 mL	(1¼ pt.)	bread crumbs

Method

1. Peel the eggplant and cut it in half lengthwise.
2. Cut the peeled eggplant into slices about 1.25 cm (½ in.) thick.
3. Place the slices in cold, salted water to prevent discolouration.
4. Drain well and bread the eggplant, using the procedure outlined on pages 111 and 112.
5. Deep fat fry at 180°C (350°F) until golden brown.
6. Drain well and serve.

Eggplant Creole   Approximate yield: 20 portions

1.8 kg	(4 lb.)	eggplant
		boiling, salted water to cover
1.5 L	(1½ qt.)	Creole sauce, hot (See Chapter 8.)
		salt and pepper to taste

Method

1. Peel the eggplant and cut it into 1.25 cm (½ in.) cubes.
2. Place the cubes in a sauce pan and add boiling, salted water to cover.
3. Simmer for 8 to 10 min, then drain well.

4. Add the hot Creole sauce to the cooked eggplant and simmer for a few minutes.
5. Season with salt and pepper to taste and serve.

Buttered Lima Beans
Approximate yield: 20 portions

1.8 kg	(4 lb.)	lima beans, frozen
		boiling, salted water to cover
180 g	(6 oz.)	butter
		salt and pepper to taste

Method

1. Place the lima beans in a sauce pan and add boiling, salted water to cover.
2. When the water returns to a boil, reduce the heat and simmer until the lima beans are tender.
3. Drain well and add butter, salt and pepper before serving.

Variation

For **creamed lima beans**, add 1.5 L (1½ qt.) of cream sauce (Chapter 8) to the cooked lima beans before serving.

Buttered Onions
Approximate yield: 20 portions

2.2 kg	(5 lb.)	small white onions, peeled
		boiling, salted water to cover
180 g	(6 oz.)	butter

Method

1. Place the peeled onions in a sauce pan and add boiling, salted water to cover.
2. Simmer the onions for approximately 30 min, or until they are tender. Do not overcook.
3. Drain the onions well and add the butter before serving.

Variation

For **creamed onions**, add 1.5 L (1½ qt.) cream sauce (Chapter 8) to the cooked onions before serving.

Buttered Peas

Approximate yield: 20 portions

1.8 kg	(4 lb.)	frozen green peas
		boiling, salted water to cover
90 g	(3 oz.)	butter
		salt and pepper to taste
		sugar to taste

Method

1. Place the peas in a sauce pan and add boiling, salted water just to cover the peas.
2. Simmer for about 5 min, or until the peas are just tender.
3. Drain the peas well and add the butter, salt, pepper and sugar before serving.

Variation

For **minted green peas**, add 60 g (2 oz.) of chopped, fresh mint to the buttered and seasoned peas before serving. 5 mL (1 tsp.) of dried mint may be substituted for fresh mint.

Buttered Spinach

Approximate yield: 20 portions

3.6 kg	(8 lb.)	fresh spinach
		boiling, salted water to cover
180 g	(6 oz.)	butter
		salt and pepper to taste

Method

1. Thoroughly wash the spinach two or three times in cold water.
2. Trim off all the stems and remove any discoloured leaves.
3. Place the spinach leaves in a large sauce pan and add boiling, salted water to barely cover the spinach.
4. Simmer until the leaves are wilted and just tender. Drain well.
5. Add the butter, salt and pepper before serving.

Variation

For **creamed spinach**, add 1.5 L (1 1/2 qt.) of cream sauce (Chapter 8) to the cooked, drained spinach. Stir in gently and season with salt and pepper to taste. Blend in the butter and serve.

Note: 2.2 kg (5 lb.) frozen spinach may be substituted for the fresh spinach.

Baked Acorn Squash
Yield: 20 portions

10		acorn squash
180 g	(6 oz.)	butter
15 mL	(1 tbsp.)	salt
180 g	(6 oz.)	brown sugar

Method

1. Wash the squash and cut them in half lengthwise. Remove the seeds.
2. Butter the cut surface of the squash lightly.
3. Place the buttered squash in a baking pan with the cut sides down.
4. Bake at 180°C (350°F) for 30 to 40 min, or until the flesh of the squash is soft.
5. Turn the squash cut side up and brush generously with butter. Season lightly with salt.
6. Sprinkle brown sugar evenly over the entire cut surface.
7. Return to the oven and cook until the sugar has melted and the squash is golden brown.
8. Serve one-half squash per portion.

Buttered Squash
Approximate yield: 20 portions

3.6 kg	(8 lb.)	squash
		boiling water
180 g	(6 oz.)	butter, melted
90 g	(3 oz.)	sugar
15 mL	(1 tbsp.)	salt
1 mL	(¼ tsp.)	pepper

Method

1. Wash and peel the squash. Remove the seeds.
2. Cut the squash in uniform pieces.
3. Place the squash in a sauce pan and add boiling water halfway to the top of the squash.
4. Cover the pan and simmer for 30 min, or until the squash is tender. Do not overcook.
5. Drain the cooked squash well and place it in the mixer.

6. Whip at low speed until the squash is broken into small pieces.
7. Add the melted butter, sugar, salt and pepper.
8. Whip at medium speed in the mixer until the lumps are gone. Do not overwhip or the squash will become watery.
9. Adjust seasonings, if necessary, and serve.

Deep-Fried Zucchini   Approximate yield: 20 portions

2.2 kg	(5 lb.)	zucchini
450 g	(1 lb.)	flour, seasoned
1 L	(1 qt.)	egg wash
675 mL	(1¼ pt.)	bread crumbs

Method

1. Wash the zucchini and trim off the ends.
2. Cut the zucchini in finger-length pieces, 1.25 cm by 5 cm (½ in. by 2 in.).
3. Place the cut pieces in cold, salted water to prevent discolouration.
4. Drain well and bread the zucchini, using the procedure outlined in Chapter 9 (on pages 111 and 112).
5. Deep fat fry the zucchini at 180°C (350°F) until golden brown.
6. Drain well and serve.

Zucchini with Dill Sauce   Approximate yield: 20 portions

3.6 kg	(8 lb.)	zucchini
120 g	(4 oz.)	butter
90 g	(3 oz.)	flour
1 L	(1 qt.)	sour cream
15 mL	(1 tbsp.)	sugar
45 mL	(3 tbsp.)	vinegar
60 mL	(4 tbsp.)	fresh dill, finely chopped

Method

1. Wash and peel the zucchini. Remove the seeds.
2. Cut the zucchini in julienne strips, 5 cm (2 in.) long.
3. Place the julienne strips in cold, salted water to prevent discolouration. Drain well.
4. Melt the butter in a sauce pan and add the zucchini.
5. Toss the zucchini in the butter until it is well coated.

6. Cover the pan and simmer the zucchini for about 10 min, or until it is barely tender.
7. Whisk the flour into the sour cream and pour the mixture over the zucchini.
8. Stir gently to mix and simmer for a few minutes until the sauce is smooth and thickened.
9. Gently stir in the sugar, vinegar and chopped dill.
10. Adjust the seasonings, if necessary, and serve.

Stewed Tomatoes

Approximate yield: 20 portions

2.5 L	(2½ qt.)	tomatoes, canned
360 g	(12 oz.)	onions, finely diced
225 g	(8 oz.)	celery, finely diced
90 g	(3 oz.)	butter
30 g	(1 oz.)	flour
30 g	(1 oz.)	sugar
10 mL	(2 tsp.)	basil
1 mL	(¼ tsp.)	thyme
10 mL	(2 tsp.)	salt
2 mL	(½ tsp.)	pepper

Method

1. Melt the butter in a sauté pan. Add the onions and celery.
2. Sauté until the vegetables are tender. Do not brown.
3. Add the flour to the vegetables to make a roux. Continue cooking on low heat for a few minutes, stirring constantly.
4. In another pot, combine the tomatoes, sugar, basil, thyme, salt and pepper.
5. Bring the tomatoes and spices to a boil and strain off the juice.
6. Gradually add the juice to the roux and cook until the mixture is smooth and thickened. Stir constantly.
7. Add the strained tomatoes and spices to the thickened mixture and simmer for 10 to 15 min.
8. Check the consistency and adjust the seasonings if necessary.

Baked Stuffed Tomatoes

Yield: 20 portions

20		fresh tomatoes, medium sized
180 mL	(6 oz.)	vegetable oil
		salt and pepper to taste
675 g	(1½ lb.)	cooked peas
180 g	(6 oz.)	butter, melted

Method

1. Slice off the bottom of each tomato.
2. Remove the centre of each tomato, leaving a fairly thick wall.
3. Place the tomatoes cavity side up in a baking pan.
4. Brush each tomato with vegetable oil and season with salt and pepper.
5. Bake the tomatoes in a 180°C (350°F) oven until they are just tender.
6. Fill each tomato with cooked green peas and add a little melted butter before serving.

Note: Cooked corn may be substituted for the cooked peas.

Buttered Turnips

Approximate yield: 20 portions

3.2 kg	(7 lb.)	turnips
		boiling, salted water to cover
10 mL	(2 tsp.)	sugar
180 g	(6 oz.)	butter
		salt and pepper to taste

Method

1. Peel the turnips and cut them in a 1.25 cm (½ in.) dice.
2. Place the diced turnip in a sauce pan and add boiling, salted water to cover.
3. Simmer the turnips, uncovered, until they are tender.
4. Drain well and add the sugar, butter, salt and pepper before serving.

Mashed Turnips

Approximate yield: 20 portions

2.2 kg	(5 lb.)	turnips
		boiling, salted water to cover
675 g	(1 ½ lb.)	potatoes
		boiling, salted water to cover
10 mL	(2 tsp.)	sugar
120 g	(4 oz.)	butter
		salt and pepper to taste

Method

1. Peel the turnips and cut them into uniform size pieces.
2. Place the turnips in a sauce pan and add boiling, salted water to cover.

3. Simmer until the turnips are tender. Drain well.
4. Peel the potatoes and cut them into uniform size pieces.
5. Place the potatoes in a sauce pan and add boiling, salted water to cover.
6. Simmer until the potatoes are tender. Drain well.
7. Combine the cooked turnips and potatoes in a mixing machine and mash together until smooth.
8. Add the sugar, butter, salt and pepper and mix well before serving.

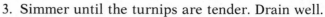

Whipped Potatoes

Approximate yield: 20 portions

3.2 kg	(7 lb.)	potatoes
		salted water to cover
120 g	(4 oz.)	butter
570 mL	(1 pt.)	milk, hot
		salt and pepper to taste

Method

1. Peel the potatoes and cut them in uniform pieces.
2. Cover the potatoes with salted water.
3. Bring to a boil, reduce the heat and cook the potatoes for 30 min, or until they are tender.
4. Drain the potatoes well and place them in a mixing machine with a paddle attachment.
5. Break up the potatoes at low speed.
6. Replace the paddle attachment with a whip attachment.
7. Beat the potatoes at low speed until they are well mashed.
8. Add the butter, hot milk, salt and pepper and beat at medium speed until all are well blended.
9. Beat at high speed until the potatoes are light and fluffy.

Duchess Potatoes

Approximate yield: 20 portions

2.7 kg	(6 lb.)	potatoes
		salted water to cover
90 g	(3 oz.)	butter, melted
5		egg yolks
		salt and pepper to taste
2 mL	(1/2 tsp.)	nutmeg, ground
250 mL	(1 cup)	eggwash

Method

1. Peel the potatoes and cut them in uniform pieces.
2. Cover the potatoes with salted water.
3. Bring to a boil, reduce the heat and cook the potatoes for 25 to 30 min, or until they are tender. Do not overcook.
4. Drain the potatoes well and place them in a mixing machine. Mix with a paddle until the potatoes are smooth.
5. Blend in the butter, egg yolks and seasonings.
6. Mix until all are well blended.
7. Place the potato mixture in a pastry bag with a star tube.
8. On a lightly buttered baking pan, pipe out the potatoes in spiral cones.
9. Brush the piped-out potatoes lightly with egg wash.
10. Brown lightly in a 220°C (425°F) oven and serve one cone per portion.

Croquette Potatoes   Approximate yield: 20 portions

2.7 kg	(6 lb.)	potatoes
		salted water to cover
90 g	(3 oz.)	butter, melted
5		egg yolks
60 g	(2 oz.)	cornstarch
		salt and pepper to taste
2 mL	(½ tsp.)	nutmeg, ground
570 mL	(1 pt.)	eggwash
675 mL	(1¼ pt.)	bread crumbs

Method

1. Peel the potatoes and cut them in uniform pieces.
2. Cover the potatoes with salted water.
3. Bring to a boil, reduce the heat and cook the potatoes for 25 to 30 min, or until they are tender. Do not overcook.
4. Drain the potatoes well and place them in a mixing machine. Mix with a paddle until the potatoes are smooth.
5. Blend in the butter, egg yolks, cornstarch and seasonings.
6. Mix until all are well blended.
7. Remove the potato mixture from the mixer.
8. Divide the potatoes into portions and form them into cylindrical shapes.

9. Bread the portions, using the breading procedure outlined in Chapter 9 (pages 111 and 112).
10. Deep fry at 180°C (350°F) until golden brown.
11. Drain well and serve.

Scalloped Potatoes   Approximate yield: 20 portions

2.7 kg	(6 lb.)	potatoes
180 g	(6 oz.)	butter
120 g	(4 oz.)	flour
2.5 L	(2½ qt.)	milk, hot
		salt and pepper to taste

Method

1. Peel the potatoes and slice them 3 mm (⅛ in.) thick.
2. Heat the butter in a sauce pan.
3. Add the flour to make a roux and cook lightly.
4. Gradually add the hot milk and whip until the cream sauce is smooth and thickened.
5. Season with salt and pepper.
6. Place the sliced potatoes in a buttered baking pan.
7. Cover with the cream sauce and bake in a 180°C (350°F) oven for 45 to 60 min, or until the potatoes are tender and the top is browned.

Oven-Roasted Potatoes   Yield: 20 portions

20		potatoes, medium sized
225 g	(8 oz.)	shortening
		salt and pepper to taste

Method

1. Peel and trim the potatoes to uniform size.
2. Melt the shortening in a baking pan.
3. Dry the potatoes thoroughly and place them in the baking pan.
4. Season the potatoes with salt and pepper.
5. Bake at 200°C (400°F) for approximately 1 h, or until the potatoes are brown and tender.
6. Turn and baste the potatoes during cooking to ensure even browning.

Fondant Potatoes   Yield: 20 portions

20		potatoes, medium sized
		salted water to cover

180 g	(6 oz.)	butter, melted
570 mL	(1 pt.)	chicken stock
		salt and pepper to taste
45 mL	(3 tbsp.)	chopped parsley

Method

1. Peel the potatoes and trim them to uniform size.
2. Cook the potatoes in boiling, salted water until they are slightly undercooked.
3. Drain the potatoes well.
4. Place the potatoes in a buttered baking pan and brush them with melted butter.
5. Add a little chicken stock to prevent burning and season the potatoes with salt and pepper.
6. Bake in a 200°C (400°F) oven until tender and browned.
7. Sprinkle with chopped parsley before serving.

Hashed Brown Potatoes   Approximate yield: 20 portions

2.2 kg	(5 lb.)	potatoes, cooked
180 mL	(6 oz.)	vegetable oil
		salt and pepper to taste
30 mL	(2 tbsp.)	parsley, chopped

Method

1. Allow cooked potatoes to cool in the refrigerator overnight.
2. Use a grater to shred the cooked potatoes into small particles.
3. Heat the oil in a large fry pan.
4. Add the potatoes and season lightly with salt and pepper.
5. Cook the potatoes over high heat for a few minutes until they are heated through.
6. When the bottom has browned well, turn the complete mass of potatoes over carefully.
7. Brown the potatoes evenly and sprinkle with chopped parsley before serving.

Variations

For **O'Brien potatoes**, add a garnish consisting of bacon, green peppers and onions that have been diced and lightly cooked. Diced pimientos are added to the cooked garnish. For **Lyonnaise potatoes**, add sautéed sliced onions to the hashed brown potatoes.

score—mark with a cut

Baked Potatoes

Yield: 20 portions

20 baking potatoes

Method

1. Wash the potatoes well. Pierce each one several times with a kitchen fork to allow steam to escape during cooking.
2. Place the potatoes in a shallow baking pan and bake at 200°C (400°F) for approximately 1 h, or until the potatoes are tender.
3. When they are cooked, the potatoes will yield to light pressure.
4. **Score** each potato with a paring knife in criss-cross fashion.
5. Squeeze the potatoes near the bottom to open them for service.
6. Serve the potatoes with butter or sour cream.

Baked Stuffed Potatoes

Yield: 20 portions

20		baking potatoes
180 g	(6 oz.)	onion, diced
180 g	(6 oz.)	green pepper, diced
180 g	(6 oz.)	ham, diced
90 g	(3 oz.)	pimientos, diced
90 g	(3 oz.)	butter
120 mL	(4 oz.)	milk, warm
		salt and pepper to taste
30 mL	(2 tbsp.)	paprika

Method

1. Bake the potatoes as in the recipe above.
2. When the potatoes are cooked, cut off the top portion of each potato by cutting lengthwise.
3. Spoon out the pulp and save the skins.
4. Cook the onion and green pepper together until they are tender. Do not brown.
5. Remove them from the heat and add the ham and pimientos.
6. Place the potato pulp in a mixing machine and mix at low speed until it becomes smooth.
7. Add the butter and the cooked garnish (onion, pepper, ham and pimientos) and continue to mix until they are well blended.
8. Add the warm milk, salt and pepper and mix until the desired consistency is reached.

9. Using a pastry bag with a star tube, pipe the mixture into the potato skins.
10. Sprinkle the potatoes with paprika and bake at 180°C (350°F) until they are heated through and browned on top.

Potato Pancakes

Approximate yield: 20 portions

2.7 kg	(6 lb.)	potatoes, peeled
225 g	(8 oz.)	onions
6		eggs
180 g	(6 oz.)	pastry flour
15 mL	(1 tbsp.)	salt
2 mL	(½ tsp.)	pepper
60 g	(2 oz.)	parsley, chopped
		vegetable oil

Method

1. Grate the potatoes and onions together.
2. Strain the liquid off the grated potatoes and onions.
3. Beat the eggs lightly and blend them with the potatoes and onions.
4. Add the flour, salt, pepper and chopped parsley. Blend well.
5. Heat 6 mm (¼ in.) of oil in a frying pan.
6. Using a 60 mL (2 oz.) ladle for each pancake, pour the batter into the frying pan.
7. Brown one side of the pancake.
8. Turn the pancake and brown the other side.
9. Drain excess oil from pancakes before serving.

RICE

Although rice is a grain, not a vegetable, it is included here because it is an excellent substitute for potatoes or vegetables. Rice is available in North America in three main varieties. These are **long grain, medium grain** and **short grain**. The nutritional value of rice is determined by the amount of milling it is subjected to. Rice is milled to remove part of the outer coating of the grain. This makes it more digestible.

Rice may be purchased as brown rice, polished rice, or converted rice. **Brown rice** has the hull of the grain removed. It is unpolished and has most of the bran coating left on. It is the highest in nutritional value of the different kinds of rice. **Polished rice** has the hull and the

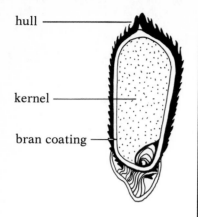

hull

kernel

bran coating

bran coating removed. This decreases its nutritional value. **Converted rice** is treated with steam before it is processed. This forces many of the nutrients, found in the outer layers of the grain, into the centre of the rice where they are not lost by polishing. Converted rice maintains good shape and texture when cooked and is therefore preferred for use in the commercial kitchen.

There are two methods of rice preparation usually practised in the commercial kitchen. The **boiling and steaming method** produces light and fluffy rice. The rice is cooked in simmering water in a covered pot until it is almost tender. It is then drained and cooked over very low heat until all excess water has evaporated. For this method, use 1 part rice to 2½ to 3 parts water.

The **pilaf method** uses a ratio of 1 part rice to 2 parts stock or water. Finely diced onions are sautéed and the rice is added to them. When all the grains of rice are coated with fat, hot stock or water is added and the pot is covered. Usually the rice is then cooked in the oven until all the liquid is absorbed and the rice is light and the grains separate.

The boiling and steaming method is primarily used when preparing rice for desserts. The pilaf method is commonly used in most other types of recipes.

Rice Pilaf
Approximate yield: 20 portions

750 mL	(3 cups)	rice, washed
150 g	(5 oz.)	onions, finely diced
150 g	(5 oz.)	butter
1.5 L	(1½ qt.)	chicken stock, hot
1		bay leaf
		salt and pepper to taste

Method

1. Melt the butter in a braising pot.
2. Add the onions and sauté for a few minutes without browning them.
3. Add the rice and continue to sauté until all the rice is coated with butter.
4. Add the chicken stock, bay leaf, salt and pepper.
5. Bring the pot to a boil and cover it.
6. Bake in a 200°C (400°F) oven for approximately 20 min, or until the rice is tender. Remove the bay leaf.
7. Remove the rice to a serving pan and stir in some butter before serving.

Spanish Rice

Approximate yield: 20 portions

360 g	(12 oz.)	rice, washed
180 g	(6 oz.)	onions, finely diced
120 g	(4 oz.)	green peppers, small dice
120 g	(4 oz.)	celery, small dice
1 L	(1 qt.)	chicken stock, hot
120 g	(4 oz.)	butter
1		bay leaf
1 L	(1 qt.)	tomatoes, canned
		salt and pepper to taste
60 g	(2 oz.)	pimientos, small dice

Method

1. Melt the butter in a braising pot.
2. Add the onions, green pepper and celery and sauté them for a few minutes without browning them.
3. Add the rice and continue to sauté until all the rice is well coated with butter.
4. Add the chicken stock, bay leaf, tomatoes, salt and pepper.
5. Bring the pot to a boil and cover it.
6. Bake in a 200°C (400°F) oven for approximately 20 min, or until the rice is tender. Remove the bay leaf.
7. Remove the rice to a serving pan and stir in the pimientos with some butter before serving.

Find the Answers to These Questions

1. In what forms can vegetables be purchased?
2. What are dried vegetables mostly used for?
3. How are vegetables classified? List the four classes of vegetables.
4. How should green vegetables be cooked to protect their colour?
5. Why is baking soda not recommended for use in cooking green vegetables?
6. What can liquid that vegetables were cooked in be used for?
7. What is the result of cooking vegetables in too much water?

CHAPTER 13
SALADS

Watch for These Words

combination	texture	palate
prior	resemble	emulsion
detract	harmony	

How to Use These Words

1. The flavour of a salad dressing must be agreeable to the __XXXX__.
2. Mayonnaise is an __XXXX__ of oil, eggs, vinegar and seasonings.
3. The leaves of Chinese cabbage __XXXX__ the leaves of romaine lettuce.
4. __XXXX__ of combined ingredients is important in the preparation of a pleasing salad.
5. A salad is a __XXXX__ of cold ingredients.
6. Important factors in salad preparation include eye appeal, colour contrast, __XXXX__, flavour and harmony of ingredients.
7. A garnish should not __XXXX__ from the body of the salad.
8. To maintain the crisp, fresh texture of a salad, the dressing should be added just __XXXX__ to service.

A salad is a **combination** of cold ingredients, usually served with some form of dressing. Salads are very wholesome and provide us with vitamins and minerals necessary for good nutrition. Salads are best classified by the main ingredients used. Most salads fit into one of the following categories:

    green leaf
    vegetable
    fruit
    meat
    seafood
    gelatin

combination—something mixed or brought together

Salads may be served as side dishes which accompany other foods. A heavy entrée requires a light salad, while a light entrée should have a heavy salad. A salad may also be served as the main course of a meal.

A leafy green salad (Courtesy of the Ontario Ministry of Agriculture and Food)

Any salad can be broken down into four component parts. These are the base, the body, the dressing and the garnish. The **base** of a salad is usually composed of lettuce or some other salad green. This is used to keep the finished salad from looking bare. Also, it provides contrast with the other ingredients. The **body** is the main part of the salad. The ingredients used in the body often give the salad its name. **A dressing** is usually served with all salads. It may be placed on the salad or mixed in with it just **prior** to serving. Adding the dressing just before serving ensures that the salad will maintain its crisp and fresh texture and appearance. The **garnish** is the finishing touch to the salad. It should provide eye appeal and a contrast to the other ingredients in the salad. The garnish should attract attention yet not **detract** from the body of the salad. The flavour and **texture** of the garnish should be related to the body of the salad.

prior—before

detract—to take away
texture—the appearance or feel of the surface

SALAD GREENS

Salad greens refer to the leafy green vegetables used in salad preparation. These include head or iceberg lettuce, romaine, escarole, Belgian endive, chicory or curly endive, Boston lettuce, spinach, Chinese cabbage, watercress and parsley.

Head or iceberg lettuce is the most common salad green. It has a firm, compact head with mild-flavoured, pale green leaves. Head lettuce retains its crispness very well. It is used for hearts of lettuce, as a base and in a variety of mixed salads.

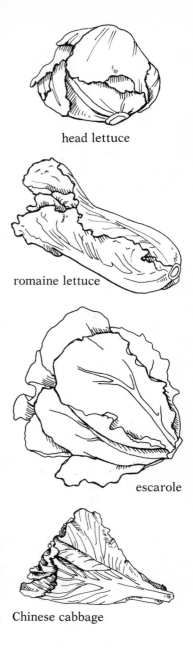

head lettuce

romaine lettuce

escarole

Chinese cabbage

Romaine lettuce has an elongated head with green leaves that are loosely packed. The outer leaves are fairly coarse. Inner leaves are pale green to cream coloured and retain their crispness well. They are used for mixed green salads and for Caesar salad.

Escarole has a flat, fan-shaped head with loose, broad leaves. It is quite bitter tasting and is best blended with sweeter, milder greens in mixed salads.

Belgian endive has smooth, cream-coloured leaves that are tightly packed to form a narrow, pointed head. It is relatively expensive and is usually served alone with a dressing. Because it is tightly packed, it should be split in half lengthwise for washing.

Chicory or curly endive has thin, twisted leaves which grow in a loosely layered bunch. The leaves are curly at the edges. Outside leaves are dark green, while the inner leaves are pale yellow. This bitter-tasting salad green is best blended with sweeter and milder greens. It is often used as the base or garnish for fruit salads.

Boston lettuce grows in a round, loosely packed head with smooth leaves. It is tender and mild flavoured. The leaves are light green in colour. Boston lettuce is usually blended in mixed salads with other salad greens. The cup-shaped leaves also serve well as a base for other salads. Boston lettuce does not keep well.

Spinach has coarse, dark green leaves and is mild in flavour. It has long, tough stems which should be removed. The leaves add colour and flavour when they are blended in mixed salads.

Chinese cabbage has a long, narrow head with leaves that **resemble** romaine lettuce in appearance. It has pale green leaves on the outside and white inner leaves. Chinese cabbage has a crisp texture and a mild cabbage flavour. It is best blended with other salad greens in mixed salads.

resemble—be like

Watercress has tiny, round, green leaves that look like clover. It has a peppery flavour and is sometimes used in mixed green salads. It is more often used as a garnish. Watercress is **fragile** and does not keep well.

fragile—easily damaged

Parsley is a flavourful herb. It serves mainly as a garnish.

GELATIN SALADS

Gelatin salads are usually made in individual moulds. A wide range of delicious and decorative salads can be easily produced from a variety of ingredients.

In preparing gelatin salads, close attention must be paid to the **ratio** of gelatin to liquid. Too much gelatin produces a tough, rubbery salad. Too little gelatin results in a runny, sloppy salad. When using fruit-flavoured gelatin, use 210 g (7 oz.) of gelatin for 1 L (1 qt.) of liquid. When using unflavoured gelatin, use 30 g (1 oz.) of gelatin for 1 L (1 qt.) of liquid. Unflavoured gelatin should be soaked in a small amount of cold water before it is used. Fruit-flavoured gelatin does not require soaking.

In order to save time in the preparation of gelatin salads, use only enough hot liquid to dissolve the gelatin completely. After the gelatin has dissolved, the balance of the required liquid can be added cold to speed up the setting process. Gelatin sets more rapidly at cold temperatures. The longer it takes to set, the more rubbery it becomes.

Although the ratios given above can be used as basic guidelines, there are factors which may change the ratio of gelatin to liquid. Such factors as the acid or sugar content of the ingredients, the temperature and the amount of setting time required for the gelatin may make changes in the basic recipes necessary. However, practical experience will soon allow you to accurately assess the relative amounts of gelatin and liquid called for.

GUIDELINES FOR GOOD SALADS

In the preparation of salads, the quality of the finished product depends largely on the quality of the ingredients used. In addition, close attention must be paid to such factors as eye appeal, colour contrast, texture, flavour and **harmony** of combined ingredients. The following of a few simple guidelines ensures that consistently good salads are produced.
1. Always use fresh ingredients.
2. Greens should be well cleaned and crisp.
3. Use combinations that are simple but colourful.
4. Try to be artistic in your salad arrangements. Create salads that are attractive and appetizing in appearance.

ratio—the relation of two quantities

harmony—the effect of an agreeable combination

Always use fresh ingredients (Courtesy of the Ontario Ministry of Agriculture and Food)

5. Vary the form in arranging salads. Fold, roll, and mound ingredients whenever possible. Flat salads are dull and unattractive.
6. Always present a salad that is properly chilled.

SALAD DRESSINGS

Successful salads depend a great deal on the quality of the dressings used. The flavour of the dressing is usually the first taste that the **palate** encounters. Thus, it is important that the first taste is an agreeable one. This may be ensured by using high quality ingredients and being extremely careful in the preparation of the dressing. There are three basic types of salad dressings. They are French, mayonnaise and boiled dressing.

palate—sense of taste

French Dressing

French dressing is an **emulsion** of oil, acids and seasonings. The acid used is usually vinegar, but lemon or lime juice may be substituted for all or part of the vinegar. French dressing is a temporary emulsion because the oil and the acid separate soon after mixing. A permanent emulsion may be obtained by using egg yolk, which keeps the oil in suspension. French dressing made with a permanent emulsion is thick and will coat the salad ingredients better than a dressing made with a temporary emulsion.

emulsion—a liquid mixture in which very tiny particles of a fatty substance are suspended

Mayonnaise

Mayonnaise is a semisolid dressing prepared by forming an emulsion of salad oil, whole eggs or egg yolks, vinegar or lemon juice and seasonings. Mayonnaise is the basis for many other dressings such as blue cheese, Thousand Island and Green Goddess.

Boiled Dressing

Boiled dressing is used in the preparation of some fruit salads, cole slaws and potato salads. It is prepared in a double boiler and contains eggs, vinegar, seasonings and cream, milk or water. Boiled dressing is thickened with cornstarch or flour.

RECIPES

Leafy Green Salads

Mixed Green Salad   Approximate yield: 20 portions

3 heads	iceberg lettuce
2 heads	romaine lettuce
2 heads	Boston lettuce
1 head	escarole
40	tomato wedges

Method

1. Wash and clean all the greens well.
2. Dry them well and keep them crisp in the refrigerator.
3. Cut or break the greens into bite-size pieces.
4. Place the greens in a mixing bowl and toss them together gently.
5. Serve each salad with two tomato wedges and an appropriate dressing such as vinaigrette, Thousand Island, Italian, or blue cheese.

Garden Salad   Approximate yield: 20 portions

3 heads	iceberg lettuce
2 heads	romaine lettuce
3 heads	Boston lettuce
1 bunch	radishes
1	cucumber
1 bunch	green onions
1/2 bunch	celery

2	carrots
40 slices	tomato
20	green pepper rings

Method

1. Wash and clean all the greens thoroughly. Drain them well and crisp them in the refrigerator.
2. Wash, trim and slice the radishes.
3. Score the cucumber with a fork. Cut it in half lengthwise and slice thinly across.
4. Trim, wash and dice the green onions.
5. Trim and wash the celery. Slice thinly across on an angle.
6. Trim, peel and wash the carrots. Shred the carrots on a grater.
7. Cut or tear the lettuces into bite-size pieces.
8. Place the lettuces in a mixing bowl and toss them together gently.
9. Add the radishes, cucumber, green onions, celery and carrots. Toss gently again.
10. Serve each portion with a garnish of two tomato slices and one green pepper ring.
11. Serve with any appropriate dressing, for example vinaigrette, Thousand Island, Italian or blue cheese.

Garden salad (Courtesy of the Ontario Ministry of Agriculture and Food)

Caesar Salad

Approximate yield: 20 portions

1.4 kg	(3 lb. or approx. 5 heads)	romaine lettuce
15 mL	(1 tbsp.)	garlic, chopped
750 mL	(3 cups)	vegetable oil
180 g	(6 oz.)	bread, cubed
180 mL	(6 oz.)	lemon juice
10 mL	(2 tsp.)	salt
1 mL	(¼ tsp.)	black pepper
20		anchovy fillets, diced
4		eggs
120 g	(4 oz.)	Parmesan cheese, grated
120 g	(4 oz.)	bacon, cooked crisp, diced

Method

1. Wash the romaine carefully and cut it into bite-size pieces. Drain the lettuce and dry it well.
2. Sauté the chopped garlic in 180 mL (6 oz.) of the vegetable oil until it is lightly browned.
3. Discard the garlic and sauté the bread cubes in the garlic-flavoured oil until they are golden brown.
4. Drain the bread cubes.
5. Combine the remaining vegetable oil, lemon juice, salt, pepper and the diced anchovy fillets to make the dressing.
6. Place the romaine lettuce in a mixing bowl. Beat the eggs slightly and add them to the lettuce.
7. Toss the lettuce gently to coat it with the egg.
8. Add the grated Parmesan cheese and toss gently again.
9. Add the dressing and mix the salad lightly.
10. Garnish with the croutons and the diced bacon bits.
11. Serve immediately.

Vegetable Salads

Green Bean with Bacon Salad

Approximate yield: 20 portions

1.8 kg	(4 lb.)	frozen green beans
180 g	(6 oz.)	onions, cut in julienne
180 g	(6 oz.)	canned pimientos, cut in julienne
5 mL	(1 tsp.)	minced garlic
750 mL	(3 cups)	basic French dressing (page 189)
360 g	(12 oz.)	bacon, cut in julienne
20		iceberg lettuce leaves
60 g	(2 oz.)	chopped parsley

A vegetable salad (Courtesy of the Ontario Ministry of Agriculture and Food)

Method

1. Cook the frozen green beans in boiling, salted water.
2. Drain the beans and let them cool.
3. Add the onions, pimientos, minced garlic and French dressing to the cooked beans.
4. Allow to stand and marinate for at least 2 h.
5. Cook the julienne bacon strips until they are crisp. Drain and allow them to cool.
6. Place a lettuce leaf on each of the cold salad plates.
7. Place a mound of the salad in the centre of each lettuce leaf.
8. Sprinkle bacon over each salad and garnish with chopped parsley.

Asparagus and Tomato Salad

Approximate yield:
20 portions

20 Boston lettuce leaves
20 thick tomato slices
60 asparagus spears, canned or fresh cooked
20 strips of canned pimientos
20 parsley sprigs

Method

1. Place a lettuce leaf on each of twenty chilled salad plates.

2. Place a thick slice of tomato in the centre of each salad plate.
3. Place three asparagus spears on top of each tomato slice.
4. Lay a strip of pimiento across the asparagus tips and garnish with a parsley sprig.
5. Serve with a vinaigrette or Italian dressing.

Cole Slaw   Approximate yield: 20 portions

1.8 kg	(4 lb. or approx. 3 medium heads)	cabbage, shredded
450 g	(1 lb.)	carrots, peeled and grated
60 g	(2 oz.)	onions, minced
480 mL	(16 oz.)	mayonnaise
120 mL	(4 oz.)	vinegar
30 g	(1 oz.)	sugar
15 mL	(1 tbsp.)	salt
2 mL	(½ tsp.)	white pepper
60 g	(2 oz.)	chopped parsley
20		dill pickle slices

Method

1. Mix the cabbage, carrots and onions together.
2. Blend the mayonnaise, vinegar, sugar, salt and white pepper together in a separate bowl.
3. Pour the dressing over the cabbage mixture.
4. Toss gently until the ingredients are well mixed.
5. Refrigerate for at least 2 h before serving.
6. Garnish each portion with a slice of dill pickle and chopped parsley.

Seafood Salads
Salmon Salad   Approximate yield: 20 portions

1.8 kg	(4 lb.)	salmon, canned, drained and flaked
900 g	(2 lb.)	celery, finely diced
60 g	(2 oz.)	onion, minced
		juice of two lemons
750 mL	(3 cups)	mayonnaise
		salt and pepper to taste
20		lettuce leaves
20		lemon wedges
20		parsley sprigs

Method

1. Place the salmon, celery and onion in a mixing bowl and toss lightly.
2. Add the lemon juice and mayonnaise and mix gently.
3. Season to taste with salt and pepper.
4. Place each lettuce leaf on a chilled salad plate.
5. Place a mound of the salad in the centre of each lettuce leaf.
6. Garnish with a lemon wedge and a parsley sprig.

Shrimp Salad   Approximate yield: 20 portions

1.8 kg	(4 lb.)	salad shrimp, cooked, peeled and deveined
675 g	(1 ½ lb.)	celery, finely diced
225 g	(8 oz.)	green pepper, finely diced
		juice of two lemons
750 mL	(3 cups)	mayonnaise
		salt and pepper to taste
20		lettuce leaves
20		lemon wedges

Method

1. Place the shrimp, celery and green pepper in a mixing bowl and toss lightly.
2. Add the lemon juice and mayonnaise and toss lightly a second time.
3. Season with salt and pepper to taste.
4. Place each lettuce leaf on a chilled salad plate.
5. Place a mound of the salad in the centre of each lettuce leaf.
6. Garnish with a lemon wedge.

Crabmeat Salad   Approximate yield: 20 portions

1.8 kg	(4 lb.)	cooked crabmeat, flaked
900 g	(2 lb.)	celery, finely diced
		juice of two lemons
750 mL	(3 cups)	mayonnaise
		salt and pepper to taste
20		lettuce leaves
20		lemon wedges
20		parsley sprigs

Method

1. Place the crabmeat and celery in a mixing bowl and toss lightly.
2. Add the lemon juice and mayonnaise and toss lightly a second time.
3. Season with salt and pepper to taste.
4. Place each lettuce leaf on a chilled salad plate.
5. Place a mound of the salad in the centre of each lettuce leaf.
6. Garnish with a lemon wedge and a sprig of parsley.

Fruit Salads

Waldorf Salad

Approximate yield: 20 portions

1.4 kg	(3 lb.)	eating apples, diced medium
450 g	(1 lb.)	celery, diced medium
		juice of one lemon
625 mL	(2½ cups)	mayonnaise
120 g	(4 oz.)	walnuts, coarsely chopped
		salt and pepper to taste
20		lettuce leaves
40		mandarin orange sections, canned

Method

1. Place the apples, celery and lemon juice in a mixing bowl and toss lightly.
2. Add the mayonnaise and chopped walnuts. Toss lightly a second time until the salad is thoroughly mixed.
3. Season with salt and pepper to taste.
4. Place each lettuce leaf on a chilled salad plate.
5. Place a mound of the salad in the centre of each lettuce leaf.
6. Garnish with two mandarin orange sections.

Orange and Grapefruit Salad

Approximate yield: 20 portions

20 lettuce leaves
60 fresh orange sections
60 fresh grapefruit sections
20 watercress sprigs

Method

1. Place each lettuce leaf on a chilled salad plate.
2. Alternate orange and grapefruit sections attractively on the lettuce leaf. Use three orange sections and three grapefruit sections for each salad.
3. Serve with a French dressing or a boiled dressing.
4. Garnish each salad with a watercress sprig.

Peach and Cottage Cheese Salad

Approximate yield: 20 portions

20		lettuce leaves
1.1 kg	(2½ lb.)	cottage cheese
20		large canned peach halves, cut in half
20		red maraschino cherries
20		mint sprigs

Method

1. Place each lettuce leaf on a chilled salad plate.
2. Place a scoop of cottage cheese in the centre of each lettuce leaf.
3. Place a wedge of peach on two sides of the cottage cheese.
4. Place a maraschino cherry on top of the cottage cheese and garnish with a sprig of mint.

Meat Salads

Chicken Salad

Approximate yield: 20 portions

1.1 kg	(2½ lb.)	chicken or turkey meat, cooked and diced into 1.25 cm (½ in.) cubes
560 g	(1¼ lb.)	celery, diced
		juice of one lemon
360 mL	(12 oz.)	mayonnaise
		salt and pepper to taste
20		lettuce leaves
20		parsley sprigs
20		pimiento strips

Method

1. Place the diced chicken and celery in a mixing bowl.
2. Add the lemon juice and mayonnaise. Toss lightly to blend the ingredients.
3. Season to taste with salt and pepper. Toss lightly again.
4. Place each lettuce leaf on a chilled salad plate.
5. Place a mound of the salad in the centre of each lettuce leaf.
6. Garnish with a strip of pimiento and a parsley sprig.

Beef and Pepper Salad   Approximate yield: 20 portions

1.1 kg	(2 ½ lb.)	cold roast beef, cut in julienne
2		green peppers, cut in julienne
2		pimientos, cut in julienne
1		onion, cut in julienne
225 mL	(8 oz.)	basic French dressing (page 189)
20		lettuce leaves
20		tomato wedges
20		parsley sprigs

Method

1. Place the roast beef, green peppers, pimientos and onion in a mixing bowl and toss gently to mix the ingredients.
2. Add the French dressing and toss lightly a second time.
3. Place each lettuce leaf on a chilled salad plate.
4. Place a mound of the salad in the centre of each lettuce leaf.
5. Garnish with a tomato wedge and a parsley sprig.

Ham Salad   Approximate yield: 20 portions

1.1 kg	(2 ½ lb.)	cooked ham, cut in julienne
560 g	(1 ¼ lb.)	celery, finely sliced on the diagonal
90 mL	(3 oz.)	sweet relish
360 mL	(12 oz.)	mayonnaise
		salt and pepper to taste
20		lettuce leaves
60		hard-boiled egg slices
20		parsley sprigs

Method

1. Place the ham and celery in a mixing bowl and toss lightly.
2. Add the sweet relish and mayonnaise and toss lightly a second time.
3. Season with salt and pepper to taste.
4. Place each lettuce leaf on a chilled salad plate.
5. Place a mound of the salad in the centre of each lettuce leaf.
6. Garnish with three slices of hard-boiled egg and a parsley sprig.

Gelatin Salads

Tomato Aspic   Approximate yield: 20 portions

60 g	(2 oz.)	unflavoured gelatin
480 mL	(16 oz.)	cold water
1.5 L	(1½ qt.)	tomato juice
120 g	(4 oz.)	celery, diced
120 g	(4 oz.)	onions, diced
3		whole cloves
1		bay leaf
5 mL	(1 tsp.)	dry mustard
5 mL	(1 tsp.)	salt
150 g	(5 oz.)	sugar
180 mL	(6 oz.)	lemon juice
20		lettuce leaves

Method

1. Add the gelatin to the cold water and let it stand for 5 min.
2. Place the tomato juice, celery, onions, cloves, bay leaf, dry mustard, salt and sugar in a sauce pan.
3. Bring these to a boil and simmer for 10 min.
4. Strain this tomato liquid and stir in the soaked gelatin until it is dissolved.
5. Add the lemon juice and stir.
6. Pour the liquid into individual moulds and refrigerate until firm.
7. Remove the salads from the moulds and serve on a bed of salad greens.

Lime, Pineapple and Cottage Cheese Mould

Approximate yield: 20 portions

360 g	(12 oz.)	lime-flavoured gelatin
1 L	(1 qt.)	boiling water
480 mL	(16 oz.)	cold water
480 mL	(16 oz.)	cottage cheese, drained
225 mL	(8 oz.)	pineapple, canned, crushed and drained
20		lettuce leaves

Method

1. Dissolve the lime gelatin in the boiling water.
2. Add the cold water and stir.
3. Pour gelatin to a depth of 1.25 cm (½ in.) in individual moulds.
4. Refrigerate until the gelatin in the moulds is firm.
5. Combine the cottage cheese and crushed pineapple.
6. Place a small amount of the mixture in each individual mould and cover with the remaining lime gelatin.
7. Refrigerate until firm.
8. Remove from the moulds and serve on a bed of salad greens.

Perfection Salad

Approximate yield: 20 portions

60 g	(2 oz.)	unflavoured gelatin
225 mL	(8 oz.)	cold water
1.5 L	(1½ qt.)	boiling water
10 mL	(2 tsp.)	salt
450 g	(1 lb.)	sugar
225 mL	(8 oz.)	vinegar
30 mL	(2 tbsp.)	lemon juice
120 g	(4 oz.)	green peppers, chopped
3		canned pimientos, chopped
900 g	(2 lb.)	cabbage, shredded
560 g	(1¼ lb.)	celery, finely diced

Method

1. Soak the unflavoured gelatin in the cold water for 5 min.
2. Combine the soaked gelatin, boiling water, salt and sugar in a mixing bowl. Stir until thoroughly dissolved.
3. Let cool and add the vinegar and lemon juice.

4. Chill until the gelatin is partially set.
5. Add the remaining ingredients and fold them into the gelatin.
6. Pour into individual moulds and refrigerate until the gelatin is firm.

Dressings

Basic French Dressing   Approximate yield: 1 L (1 qt.)

225 mL	(8 oz.)	vinegar
15 mL	(1 tbsp.)	salt
8 mL	(1 1/2 tsp.)	white pepper
750 mL	(3 cups)	salad oil

Method

1. Add the salt and white pepper to the vinegar and stir well to dissolve the seasonings.
2. Add the salad oil and mix vigorously to form a temporary emulsion.
3. Mix well again before serving.

Variations

Cucumber dressing: add 750 mL (3 cups) of grated cucumber to 1 L (1 qt.) of basic French dressing.
Cheese dressing: add 120 g (4 oz.) of grated cheese and 5 mL (1 tsp.) of prepared mustard to 1 L (1 qt.) of basic French dressing.
Garlic dressing: add 2 mL (1/2 tsp.) of finely mashed garlic to 1 L (1 qt.) of basic French dressing.
Herb dressing: add 2 mL (1/2 tsp.) basil, 2 mL (1/2 tsp.) tarragon, 1 mL (1/4 tsp.) marjoram and 5 mL (1 tsp.) fresh chopped parsley to 1 L (1 qt.) of basic French dressing.

Thick French Dressing   Approximate yield: 1 L (1 qt.)

150 mL	(5 oz.)	vinegar
5 mL	(1 tsp.)	salt
1 mL	(1/4 tsp.)	white pepper
5 mL	(1 tsp.)	paprika
30 g	(1 oz.)	sugar
5 mL	(1 tsp.)	dry mustard
5 mL	(1 tsp.)	Worcestershire sauce
45 mL	(3 tbsp.)	lemon juice
45 mL	(3 tbsp.)	water
1		whole egg
625 mL	(2 1/2 cups)	salad oil

Method

1. Blend together the vinegar, salt, white pepper, paprika, sugar, dry mustard, Worcestershire sauce, lemon juice and water.
2. Beat the egg in a stainless steel bowl.
3. Slowly add the salad oil to the egg while beating constantly.
4. As the egg-and-oil mixture thickens and the emulsion forms, gradually add the mixture blended in Step 1.
5. Alternate additions of salad oil and the blended mixture until all the ingredients are incorporated with the egg.
6. Check seasonings and store the dressing in the refrigerator for later use.

Creamy Italian Dressing Approximate yield: 1 L (1 qt.)

120 mL	(4 oz.)	vinegar
1 mL	(¼ tsp.)	black pepper
8 mL	(1½ tsp.)	garlic, minced
8 mL	(1½ tsp.)	salt
8 mL	(1½ tsp.)	dry mustard
8 mL	(1½ tsp.)	lemon juice
8 mL	(1½ tsp.)	Worcestershire sauce
5 mL	(1 tsp.)	tarragon
5 mL	(1 tsp.)	basil
2 mL	(½ tsp.)	sugar
15 mL	(1 tbsp.)	green onion, finely chopped
2 drops		tabasco sauce
1		whole egg
750 mL	(3 cups)	salad oil

Method

1. Blend together the vinegar, black pepper, garlic, salt, dry mustard, lemon juice, Worcestershire sauce, tarragon, basil, sugar, green onion and tabasco sauce.
2. Beat the egg in a stainless steel bowl.
3. Slowly add the salad oil to the egg while beating constantly.
4. As the egg-and-oil mixture thickens and the emulsion forms, gradually add the mixture blended in Step 1.
5. Alternate additions of salad oil and the blended mixture until all the ingredients are incorporated with the egg.

6. Check seasonings and store the dressing in the refrigerator for later use.

Mayonnaise
Approximate yield: 1 L (1 qt.)

4		egg yolks (room temperature)
10 mL	(2 tsp.)	dry mustard
10 mL	(2 tsp.)	salt
15 mL	(1 tbsp.)	sugar
875 mL	(3½ cups)	salad oil (room temperature)
60 mL	(2 oz.)	vinegar
30 mL	(2 tbsp.)	lemon juice

Method
1. Beat the egg yolks in a stainless steel bowl.
2. Mix the dry mustard, salt and sugar together and add them to the beaten egg yolk.
3. Beat until the dry ingredients are incorporated with the egg yolks.
4. Slowly add the salad oil while beating constantly.
5. When the mixture thickens, add a small amount of the vinegar.
6. Alternate additions of oil and vinegar until both are used up.
7. Add the lemon juice.

Thousand Island Dressing
Approximate yield: 1 L (1 qt.)

500 mL	(2 cups)	mayonnaise
225 mL	(8 oz.)	chili sauce
30 mL	(2 tbsp.)	pimientos, finely chopped
30 mL	(2 tbsp.)	onion, minced
120 mL	(4 oz.)	sweet pickled relish
2		hard-boiled eggs, chopped
30 mL	(2 tbsp.)	parsley, finely chopped

Method
1. Combine all ingredients and mix well.

Variation
For Russian dressing, add 60 mL (2 oz.) caviar.

Green Goddess Dressing

Approximate yield: 1 L (1 qt.)

570 mL	(1 pt.)	mayonnaise
225 mL	(8 oz.)	sour cream
30 mL	(2 tbsp.)	**anchovies**, minced
8 mL	(1½ tsp.)	garlic, minced
60 g	(2 oz.)	parsley, minced
30 mL	(2 tbsp.)	green onions, minced
5 mL	(1 tsp.)	salt
1 mL	(¼ tsp.)	black pepper
30 mL	(2 tbsp.)	vinegar
45 mL	(3 tbsp.)	lemon juice

Method

1. Combine all ingredients in a stainless steel bowl and blend thoroughly.

Blue Cheese Dressing

Approximate yield: 1 L (1 qt.)

225 g	(8 oz.)	blue cheese
500 mL	(2 cups)	mayonnaise
2 mL	(½ tsp.)	dry mustard
1 mL	(¼ tsp.)	salt
1 mL	(¼ tsp.)	white pepper
60 mL	(2 oz.)	vinegar
120 mL	(4 oz.)	oil
120 mL	(4 oz.)	cold water

Method

1. Crumble the cheese into small pieces in a stainless steel bowl.
2. Add the mayonnaise and blend well.
3. Dissolve the mustard, salt and pepper in the vinegar.
4. Add the oil to the mayonnaise and cheese while beating constantly.
5. Blend in the vinegar and dissolved seasonings.
6. Add the cold water and mix thoroughly.

Boiled Dressing

Approximate yield: 1 L (1 qt.)

120 g	(4 oz.)	flour
60 g	(2 oz.)	sugar
15 mL	(1 tbsp.)	salt
20 mL	(4 tsp.)	dry mustard
5		whole eggs
750 mL	(3 cups)	milk
150 mL	(5 oz.)	vinegar
60 g	(2 oz.)	butter

anchovy—small, herring-like fish found in warm seas

Method

1. Blend together the flour, sugar, salt and dry mustard.
2. Add the eggs and beat until smooth.
3. Add the milk and mix well.
4. Add the vinegar slowly.
5. Cook in a double boiler over low heat.
6. Stir constantly until the mixture is thick.
7. Remove from the heat and whip in the butter.
8. Cool well before serving.

Find the Answers to These Questions

1. What are the component parts of a salad?
2. What are the functions of the garnish in a salad?
3. Five factors must always be considered in the preparation of salads. List these factors.
4. Before unflavoured gelatin can be used, what should you do?
5. How is a permanent emulsion achieved in a salad dressing?
6. Mayonnaise is the basis for many other salad dressings. List three such dressings.

CHAPTER 14
BREAKFAST COOKERY

Watch for These Words

function	versatile	mushy
aspiring	invert	steeping
weep	convenient	dilute

How to Use These Words

1. When the omelet was cooked, the chef took a spatula to __XXXX__ it and put it on a warm plate.
2. Eggs are very __XXXX__ because they can be used for many different preparations.
3. Restaurants normally use stainless steel pots for __XXXX__ tea.
4. To __XXXX__ strong tea, add hot water.
5. Good nutrition helps the body to __XXXX__ at a high rate of efficiency.
6. Overcooking the fruit resulted in a __XXXX__ product.
7. If too much liquid is used in scrambled eggs, they will __XXXX__ after cooking.
8. The __XXXX__ chef studied hard for her final examination.
9. The microwave oven is very __XXXX__ for defrosting food.

As the first meal consumed after a fast of almost twelve hours, breakfast is extremely important nutritionally. The body needs a balanced breakfast in order to **function** at peak efficiency throughout the day. The **aspiring** cook should have a thorough knowledge of the egg, meat, potato, batter, cereal and fruit dishes which are part of breakfast cookery.

function—to perform as required

aspiring—having an earnest desire or ambition

EGGS

Eggs are a complete protein food. They provide the body with amino acids, vitamins, fat and iron. They are easy to

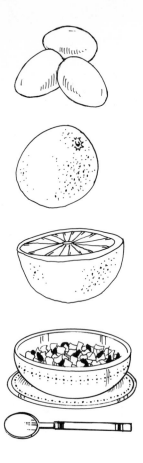

digest if they are properly cooked. In addition to being a popular breakfast item, eggs are an excellent meat substitute and are often used as a main course at lunch and dinner.

In Canada, eggs are graded according to cleanliness, shape and quality. The grade A egg is the most common one used in restaurant kitchens. Grade B and grade C eggs are usually reserved for use in bakeries. Eggs are also classified according to size. The size classifications are:

extra large	67.5 g	(2.25 oz.)
large	60.0 g	(2 oz.)
medium	52.5 g	(1.75 oz.)
small	45.0 g	(1.5 oz.)
peewee less than	45.0 g	(1.5 oz.)

Eggs have porous shells that allow strong, undesirable odours to be absorbed quickly. Therefore, eggs should always be refrigerated in closed containers to minimize the risk of having them absorb unwanted odours.

EGG COOKERY

Fried Eggs

Always fry eggs to order. Use high quality eggs and cook them in butter, margarine or shortening. The fat should be hot enough to set the eggs but not so hot as to brown the whites. Carefully break the eggs, one at a time, into a small dish and then slide them into a hot greased pan or onto a griddle. Cook the eggs as requested by the customer. **Sunny-side-up** eggs are not turned over. **Basted** eggs have hot fat spooned over them or are covered while they are cooking. **Over-easy eggs** are turned over carefully and cooked briefly on the other side. Always use a slotted spatula to remove the cooked eggs from the pan or griddle. This allows excess fat to drain off the eggs.

Scrambled Eggs

Scrambled eggs should be soft and fluffy. They require very little cooking. Overcooked scrambled eggs are dry and hard. Break the eggs into a bowl and beat them lightly with a fork or wire whisk. A small amount of cold water, cream or milk may be added. Do not use more than 15 mL (1 tbsp.) of liquid for every two eggs. Too much liquid will cause the eggs to **weep** after cooking. Place the lightly beaten eggs in a heated, buttered pan so that they start to coagulate immediately. Stir the eggs gently with a wooden

weep—to ooze drops of liquid

spoon until they are cooked to the desired consistency. Remove the eggs from the heat and serve immediately.

The eggs will continue to cook for a short time after they are removed from the heat. Large quantities of scrambled eggs are best cooked in a double boiler. They should be stirred constantly with a wooden spoon to ensure uniform cooking and to avoid lumpiness. Once the eggs are cooked to a creamy consistency, they are removed from the heat and transferred to another warm container for holding and service. For extended holding time, a small amount of cream can be mixed into the scrambled eggs after they are cooked. This stops the cooking process of the eggs by quickly reducing their temperature.

Boiled or Simmered Eggs

Although the common term is "boiled eggs," eggs should never be boiled. For best results they should be simmered at a temperature of approximately 90.6°C (195°F). The eggs should be at room temperature before they are placed in hot water. This will reduce the possibility of the eggs cracking when they are placed in the hot water. Eggs that are left in the refrigerator until it is time to cook them should be placed in warm running water before they are placed in the hot water.

There are two methods of simmering eggs. For **the boiling water method**, you place the eggs in boiling water. Reduce the heat to simmer the eggs to the desired degree of doneness. For soft-cooked eggs, allow 3 to 5 min; for medium-cooked eggs, allow 7 to 8 min; for hard-cooked eggs, allow 12 to 15 min. With **the cold water method**, you place the eggs in cold water. Bring the water to a boil and then reduce the heat to simmer and cook the eggs to the desired degree of doneness. For soft-cooked eggs, allow about 1 min; for medium-cooked eggs, allow 3 to 5 min; for hard-cooked eggs, allow 8 to 10 min.

If eggs are hard cooked and stored for later use, they should be thoroughly cooled in cold water immediately after cooking. This releases the pressure between the egg whites and the shell and allows gases, which can discolour the eggs, to escape.

Poached Eggs

Water used for poaching eggs should be salted and acidified by adding 5 mL (1 tsp.) salt and 15 mL (1 tbsp.) vinegar for every litre (or quart) of water. This helps to set the egg white firmly around the yolk when the egg is placed in the water.

Fill a fairly shallow pan with enough acidified water to cover the eggs completely. Bring the water to a boil and keep it at the simmering point. Break the eggs into a bowl or saucer and gently slide the eggs into the simmering water. Cook as desired: 3 to 5 min is usually sufficient cooking time. Remove the eggs with a skimmer or perforated spoon and drain them well before serving on hot buttered toast.

For larger quantities of poached eggs, poach the eggs just until the white is set and the eggs are firm enough to remove from the water. Immediately place the cooked eggs in cold water to stop the cooking process. The eggs can then be reheated in hot, salted water as they are needed.

Shirred Eggs

shirred—baked in a buttered dish

Break two eggs into a saucer or bowl. Gently transfer the eggs to a buttered **shirred**-egg dish. Place the dish on top of the range and cook over medium heat until the whites are set. Finish cooking in the oven at 160°C (325°F). Cooked bacon, sausage, ham or chicken livers can be placed around the edge of the shirred-egg dish before serving.

Omelets

versatile—able to be used in many different ways

invert—turn upside down

Omelets are popular items on breakfast and luncheon menus. They are **versatile** because they blend well with other foods. Different fillings make a wide variety of omelets possible. Popular omelet fillings are bacon, ham, cheese, Spanish sauce and mushrooms. When a particular filling is used, the omelet takes on the name of the filling. Examples of this are Spanish omelets or mushroom omelets. Omelets should be made to order. They do not hold well, quickly losing their lightness and becoming rubbery and tough. Omelets are usually served either rolled or folded.

For a **rolled omelet**, break three eggs into a mixing bowl and beat lightly with a wire whisk or a fork. Place the egg mixture in a well-greased, hot egg skillet. As the eggs bubble in the pan, tilt it in all directions to completely cover the surface of the pan. Reduce the heat and cook the egg mixture at moderate heat. As the eggs are cooking, use a palette knife (or spatula) to lift the cooked portion slightly from the sides of the pan. Tilt the pan to allow the remaining liquid portion of the egg to run to the side. When the eggs are slightly set but still moist, tilt the pan and use a palette knife to start rolling the egg away from you. When the omelet is rolled, **invert** it carefully on a warm plate.

Cover the omelet with a clean cloth to absorb excess grease and to shape the omelet.

For a **folded omelet**, follow the same procedure as used with the rolled omelet until the eggs are set but still moist. Tilt the pan and use a palette knife to carefully fold the omelet in half. Invert the omelet on a warm plate.

If a filling is used in the omelet, it is placed in the centre of the omelet just before rolling or folding.

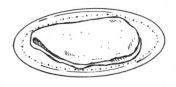

BREAKFAST MEATS

Bacon, ham and sausages are the most popular breakfast meats. Bacon and ham are cured by smoking, while sausage meat is fresh. When customer volume is large, they are usually blanched or precooked prior to serving.

Bacon may be purchased in slabs which are sliced in the kitchen, or it may be purchased already sliced and ready to cook. To precook bacon, the slices are separated and placed on a baking sheet with the slices overlapping each other. The bacon is placed in a 180°C (350°F) oven and cooked until about three-quarters done. The accumulated fat is poured off and the bacon is transferred to a smaller pan lined with absorbent towels. Cooking is then completed on the grill, to order, as required. This method of cooking bacon reduces shrinkage and curling, improves the appearance and cooks the bacon more uniformly. When smaller quantities of bacon are needed, they may be cooked in a frying pan on the range or grilled on the griddle.

Breakfast **ham** is usually purchased cooked and boneless. Boneless hams have a uniform shape which makes portion control easier. Since ham is already cooked, it is simply a matter of heating it on the griddle or in a frying pan before serving.

Breakfast **sausage** is considered a fresh pork product and should always be cooked well done. It is available in **sausage links** or in **sausage patties**. Link sausages may be blanched for quantity service. Place the sausages in cold water and bring them to a boil. Remove the sausages from the heat and cool them completely under cold running water. They can then be separated and refrigerated for later use.

Blanching link sausages prevents splitting of the sausage casing, removes excess fat from the sausages and helps to retain moisture when they are finally cooked for service. Smaller quantities of link sausages can be partially baked on baking sheets at 180°C (350°F), grilled on a griddle, or cooked in a frying pan on the range. Only cook the sausages until the links are about three-quarters done. Then drain off excess fat and finish cooking the sausages as they are needed for serving. Sausage patties have no outer casing and so they cannot be blanched in water. However, any of the other methods outlined above (baking, grilling, frying) are suitable for cooking sausage patties.

POTATOES

Potatoes served on a breakfast menu are usually fried. Popular preparations include hashed brown potatoes, O'Brien potatoes, Lyonnaise potatoes (all on page 167) and home-fried potatoes.

PANCAKES

Pancakes are a popular breakfast food. They must be cooked to order and served piping hot with fresh butter and jam, jelly or syrup. The most popular syrup is pure maple syrup, but it is fairly expensive. Instead, many establishments use a maple-flavoured syrup. A variety of fruit-flavoured syrups are also used.

convenient—easy to use

Most commercial kitchens now use prepared pancake mixes because they are so **convenient**. These mixes require the addition of water or milk. Higher quality mixes may call for the addition of milk, oil and eggs. Despite the widespread use of pancake mixes, the aspiring cook should know how to make basic pancake batters.

RECIPES

Plain Pancakes		Approximate yield: 45 pancakes
8		whole eggs
2 L	(2 qt.)	milk
360 mL	(12 oz.)	vegetable oil
900 g	(2 lb.)	all-purpose flour
150 g	(5 oz.)	sugar
15 mL	(1 tbsp.)	salt
45 mL	(3 tbsp.)	baking powder

Method

1. Crack the eggs into a mixing bowl and mix at low speed for 1 min.
2. Add the milk and the vegetable oil. Continue to mix at low speed for 1 min more.

3. In a separate bowl, combine the flour, sugar, salt and baking powder.
4. Sift the combined dry ingredients.
5. Add the sifted ingredients gradually to the liquid ingredients and mix at low speed for 1 min.
6. Scrape down the sides of the mixing bowl and transfer the batter to another bowl.
7. Allow the batter to stand for 10 min before proceeding.
8. Heat the griddle to 190°C (375°F) and grease lightly.
9. Use a 90 mL (3 oz.) ladle to pour portions of the batter onto the griddle. Leave enough space between portions, as the batter for each pancake will spread to about 12 cm (5 in.) in diameter.
10. Cook on one side until golden brown, then turn and brown the second side.
11. Serve three pancakes per order.

CEREALS

Cereals should always be on the breakfast menu. They are starches and provide a valuable source of energy in the form of carbohydrates. Most cereals are relatively low in fat content, although they vary in the amounts of protein they contain.

Cereals are usually found in two forms on the breakfast menu: ready-to-eat cereals such as corn flakes, bran and shredded wheat; and cooked cereals such as oatmeal and cream of wheat. Cooked cereals are available in two forms: quick cooking and regular. Quick-cooking cereal has been precooked and therefore can be prepared more quickly than regular cooked cereal. When preparing cooked cereals, always refer to the cooking directions provided on the package.

FRUITS

Fruits are popular breakfast menu items. Fresh fruits such as oranges and grapefruit are available all year round, while different varieties of melons can be served in season. Melons should be ripe and chilled before serving. Depending on their size, melons are served in halves or in wedges.

Dried fruits such as apricots, figs and prunes can be **stewed** and served for breakfast. Do not overcook dried fruits. They should retain their shape and texture. Overcooking makes the fruit **mushy** and unattractive.

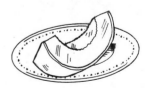

stewed—cooked slightly in water to restore their moisture
mushy—soft and shapeless

JUICES

While fruit and vegetable juices are often served at all meals, they are most popular at breakfast. Juices are available fresh, frozen or canned. The most popular juices are orange, grapefruit, apple, pineapple, tomato, prune and blends of fruit or vegetable juices. Frozen juices should be allowed to stand for a short time after mixing. This improves the flavour. All juices should be served chilled.

BEVERAGES

Coffee and tea are the most common hot beverages served with breakfast.

Coffee is made from the coffee bean, which is the green seed produced by the coffee tree. When green, the coffee bean does not spoil and so coffee is shipped from the countries where it is grown in its green form. The coffee colour, flavour and aroma are developed through the roasting of the green beans. Different varieties of roasted coffee beans are blended to produce specific desirable aromas and flavours. Coffee is usually purchased as ground coffee by food service establishments. Ground coffee should be stored in a cool, dry place because exposure to air and moisture causes coffee to become stale.

There are four general rules for making good coffee.

1. Always use clean equipment.
2. Use freshly boiled water.
3. Use fresh coffee.
4. Measure coffee and water accurately.

brewing—preparing a beverage by boiling or steeping

The two most common methods of **brewing** coffee are by using a percolator and by using a drip or filter coffee maker. In a percolator, water is drawn from the bottom of the percolator through a tube in the centre. The tube sprays the hot water evenly over the ground coffee in the basket at the top of the percolator. In the drip or filter coffee maker, a paper filter is used with coffee of a very fine grind. The hot water is in a container above the coffee grounds. It pours through a spray head, which spreads it evenly over the ground coffee, and is caught below in another container.

Brewed coffee should be kept at a temperature between 85°C and 90°C (185°F and 190°F). Holding the coffee at higher temperatures causes it to lose its flavour and become bitter. The longer brewed coffee is kept, the more flavour and aroma it loses. It is better to brew coffee more frequently and in small batches so that a fresh beverage is always served.

Tea is prepared from the leaves of the tea bush, which is grown in Asian countries. There are three major types of tea: black, green and oolong tea. They differ only in the way they are processed. In North America, black tea is the one most commonly served. For commercial service, tea is packaged in individual one- or two-cup tea bags. Although a china pot is considered best for **steeping** tea, food service establishments use stainless steel teapots for individual service.

steeping—soaking in liquid

To make good tea, three simple rules should be followed.
1. Preheat the teapot.
2. Use good quality tea.
3. Use fresh boiling water.

To make tea for individual service, preheat the teapot with boiling water. Place the tea bag in the pot and fill the pot with fresh boiling water. A second pot of hot water is usually served with the tea so that the customer can **dilute** the tea if it is too strong.

dilute—make weaker by adding water

Find the Answers to These Questions

1. Why is breakfast nutritionally important?
2. What type of food are eggs?
3. What factors are considered in the grading of eggs?
4. Why should eggs be stored in closed containers?
5. Explain the following terms for fried eggs:
   (a) sunny-side-up
   (b) basted
   (d) over-easy
6. What will happen if too much liquid is used in scrambled eggs?
7. What should you add to the water used for poaching eggs? Why?
8. How many eggs are usually contained in an omelet?
9. Describe the procedure for precooking bacon.
10. What type of food are cereals?
11. Why is the roasting of the beans so important in producing coffee?
12. Why is coffee better if it is brewed in small batches?
13. What are the three major types of tea?

CHAPTER 15
DESSERTS

Watch for These Words

creativity	key	nuggets
leavening agent	delicate	tines
considered	sift	

How to Use These Words

1. The baker had to __XXXX__ the flour before he could use it.
2. The prongs of a fork are also called __XXXX__.
3. The dessert table lacked __XXXX__ and was unappealing.
4. The method outlined by the instructor was __XXXX__ to be the easiest method.
5. Baking powder is an example of a __XXXX__.
6. A good pie crust should have a __XXXX__ taste.
7. Blending flour and shortening together will produce small __XXXX__.
8. The __XXXX__ to successful pies is a good pie crust.

Cakes, pies and many different varieties of pastries have been dessert favourites throughout time. They provide the perfect ending to a satisfying meal. The range of desserts available to the dining public is limited only by the **creativity** and imagination of those responsible for their preparation. Some of the most popular desserts, prepared mainly in the bake shop, are discussed in this chapter. Successful desserts depend largely upon the use of high quality ingredients and strict adherence to tested recipes. **Accurate measuring of ingredients is most vital in the bake shop if consistently good results are to be achieved.**

creativity—inventiveness

Strawberry shortcake (Courtesy of the Ontario Ministry of Agriculture and Food)

PUFF PASTRY DESSERTS

Puff pastry dough is different from any other type of dough. It does not contain any sugar or **leavening agent**. However, when heat is applied through the baking process, the pastry will rise to about eight times its original size. This effect is achieved by rolling and folding alternate layers of fat and dough a total of four times. Finished puff pastry has a very crisp, flaky and tender texture and is the basis for a wide variety of delicious desserts.

Great care must be taken in preparing and rolling puff pastry. Here are the rules to follow for a high quality pastry:

1. Measure ingredients carefully.
2. Prepare the dough strictly according to the recipe.
3. Butter or puff pastry shortening must have the same degree of hardness or softness as the dough before it is rolled into the dough.
4. Keep the pastry refrigerated after it is rolled.
5. Brush off all excess flour before folding the pastry.
6. Allow the pastry to rest for 20 to 30 min before folding.
7. Left-over pastry should have additional rolling before being cut into units.
8. After the pastry is cut into individual units, it should rest for 20 to 30 min before baking. This will prevent excessive shrinkage.

leavening agent—ingredient which causes dough to rise during baking

RECIPES

Puff Pastry Dough

Approximate yield: 40 turnovers

1 kg	(2 lb. 4 oz.)	bread flour
15 mL	(1 tbsp.)	salt
570 mL	(20 oz.)	water
1 kg	(2 lb. 4 oz.)	puff pastry shortening
30 g	(1 oz.)	bread flour

Method

1. Place the first three ingredients in a mixer and mix into a dough.
2. Remove the dough from the mixer and round it into a ball. Allow the dough to stand for 15 to 20 min.
3. Combine the puff pastry shortening and the 30 g (1 oz.) of bread flour. Shape into a block.
4. Roll the ball of dough into a rectangle approximately 20 cm by 30 cm (8 in. by 12 in.).
5. Place the puff pastry shortening and flour mixture on one-half of the dough and fold the second half of the dough over to cover the shortening mixture.
6. Flatten the dough by gently pounding it with a rolling pin.
7. Roll the dough out again into a rectangle 20 cm by 30 cm (8 in. by 12 in.).
8. Brush off all excess flour and make a **three-way fold** by folding one-third of the length of the dough over the middle third and folding the last third back over the middle third. This procedure is also called **the single turn.**

9. Cover the dough and allow it to stand for 20 to 30 min before rolling again.
10. Brush off all excess flour and roll the dough into a rectangle 20 cm by 30 cm (8 in. by 12 in.).
11. Make a **four-way fold** by folding both lengthwise ends to meet in the middle of the dough and then folding one-half of the dough over the other half. This procedure is also called **the double turn.**

 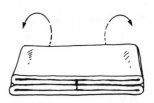

12. Allow the dough to stand for 20 to 30 min.
13. Repeat the rolling process with one more single turn and one more double turn, letting the dough stand for 20 to 30 min between turns.

It is important to remember that puff pastry must always have four turns applied in the following sequence:

1. a single turn (three-way fold)
2. a double turn (four-way fold)
3. a single turn (three-way fold)
4. a double turn (four-way fold)

Turnovers

1. Roll out puff pastry dough 3 mm (1/8 in.) thick.
2. Cut the dough into 12.5 cm (5 in.) squares.
3. Moisten the surface of the dough with water.
4. Place fruit filling in the centre of each square and fold corner-to-corner to form a triangle.
5. Seal the edges of the pastry triangles by pressing them with a fork and puncture the top of the turnover with a fork.
6. Place the turnovers on a baking sheet lined with silicone paper or greased. Allow the turnovers to stand for 30 min before baking.
7. Bake at 190°C (375°F) for 20 to 25 min.

Napoleon Slices   Yield: 48 slices

1. Roll out puff pastry dough 3 mm (1/8 in.) thick to cover a baking pan.
2. Place the dough on a 60 cm x 40 cm (24 in. x 16 in.) baking sheet and allow it to stand for 30 min.
3. Prick the dough all over with a fork to prevent blistering while baking.
4. Bake the dough at 190°C (375°F) for 20 to 25 min until it is dry and crisp but not overly browned.
5. After the puff pastry is baked, cut the sheet into three equal strips.

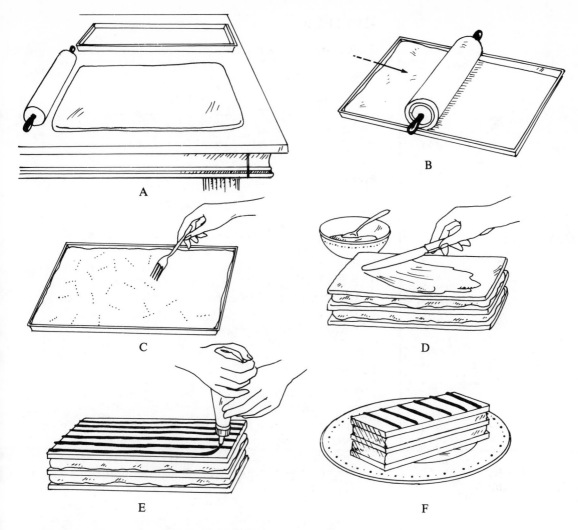

A

B

C

D

E

F

6. Place the strips on top of one another with pastry cream (page 211) between the layers.
7. Ice the top with one or more flavours of fondant icing.
8. When the fondant sets, cut the pastry carefully into bars 10 cm (4 in.) wide and 5 cm (2 in.) long.

ÉCLAIR OR CHOUX PASTE DESSERTS

Choux paste is another type of dough that does not contain a leavening agent. However, when heat is applied during the baking process, steam is created from the moisture in the choux paste. This causes the dough to expand and form crisp shells with hollow centres. A variety of fillings can be placed in these hollow centres to create interesting and delicious desserts.

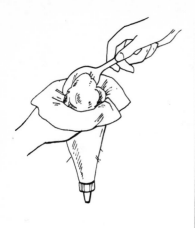

RECIPES

Éclair or Choux Paste

Approximate yield: 30 portions

570 mL	(20 oz.)	water
180 g	(6 oz.)	shortening
5 mL	(1 tsp.)	salt
360 g	(12 oz.)	bread flour
9		eggs

Method

1. Bring the water, shortening and salt to a good, rolling boil in a sauce pan.
2. Add the bread flour and cook, while stirring, until the mixture is smooth and comes cleanly away from the sides of the sauce pan. Remove from the heat.
3. Add the eggs, one or two at a time, and stir until a medium-stiff paste is obtained. Always make sure that each addition of eggs is thoroughly mixed in before adding more eggs.

Éclairs

1. Line a baking sheet with silicone paper or lightly grease the sheet.
2. Fill a pastry bag, fitted with a 1.25 cm (½ in.) plain tube, with choux paste.
3. Pipe out finger-shaped lengths of 8 to 10 cm (3 to 4 in.) on the baking sheet. Space the piped-out fingers well apart.
4. Bake at 230°C (450°F) until dry and golden brown.
5. When the éclairs are cool, they may be filled with pastry cream or whipped cream.
6. Finish the éclairs by dipping the tops in flavoured fondant icing or melted chocolate.

Swans

1. Using a plain 1.25 cm (½ in.) tube and pastry bag, pipe choux paste onto a lightly greased or paper-lined baking sheet in 5 cm (2 in.) diameter puffs. Space the puffs well apart.
2. Using a plain 6 mm (¼ in.) tube and pastry bag, pipe choux paste in question-mark shapes onto a lightly greased or paper-lined baking sheet. These question-mark shapes will form the necks and heads of the swans.

3. Bake the puffs and necks at 230°C (450°F) until they are dry and golden brown.
4. When the puff shells are cool, cut off the top third of each shell.
5. Cut these top thirds into two equal pieces to use as the wings of the swans.
6. Fill the shells with pastry cream or whipped cream and place the wings and necks in position in the filling.
7. Finish the swans by lightly dusting them with icing sugar.

French Doughnuts

1. Cut a piece of heavy paper to one-half the size of a deep fat frying kettle. Grease the paper.
2. Using a pastry bag fitted with a star tube, pipe choux paste in rings 5 to 8 cm (2 to 3 in.) in diameter on the heavy paper. Space the rings well apart.
3. Take the paper in both hands and lower it, paper side up, into the deep fat frying kettle with the temperature of the fat at 190°C (375°F).
4. The rings will drop off the paper into the hot fat and the paper can be removed.
5. Fry the doughnuts until they are golden brown on one side. Flip the doughnuts over and brown the other side.
6. When both sides are golden brown, remove the doughnuts from the fat and drain well.
7. These doughnuts are usually dipped in warm fondant icing after they have cooled.
8. Place the iced doughnuts on a wire rack to allow excess icing to run off.

Basic Pastry Cream   Approximate yield: 1 L (1 qt.)

850 mL	(1 1/2 pt.)	milk
90 g	(3 oz.)	sugar
90 g	(3 oz.)	sugar
90 g	(3 oz.)	egg yolks
45 g	(1 1/2 oz.)	soft flour
30 g	(1 oz.)	cornstarch
120 mL	(4 oz.)	milk
15 g	(1/2 oz.)	butter
5 mL	(1 tsp.)	vanilla

Method

1. Scald the 850 mL (1½ pt.) of milk mixed with 90 g (3 oz.) of sugar.
2. Combine the next five ingredients in a mixing bowl. Beat well until the mixture is very smooth.
3. Add a small amount of the scalded milk to the egg yolk mixture.
4. Mix well and add the egg yolk mixture to the rest of the scalded milk.
5. Cook and stir constantly with a wire whisk to prevent scorching and lumps in the cream.
6. When the cream is thick and smooth, remove it from the heat and add the butter and vanilla.

This basic pastry cream may be used to fill éclairs or flavoured and used as a cream filling for such pies as coconut cream, chocolate cream and banana cream.

CAKE BATTERS

The production of successful cakes depends on five essential factors. These are:
1. a good, reliable recipe
2. the use of high quality ingredients
3. careful and accurate measuring of ingredients
4. correct mixing procedures
5. correct baking procedures

Although all these factors play a vital role in the production of a good cake, most failures occur during the mixing process. Strict adherence to the mixing instructions given in the recipe is most important.

There are three recommended methods for mixing cake batters. These are:
1. the creaming method
2. the whipping method
3. the blending method

For our purposes, the blending method will be used. It is generally **considered** to be the easiest mixing method.

considered—believed, judged

RECIPES

White Cake

Yield: 6 cakes 25 cm (10 in.) in diameter

1.1 kg	(2 lb. 8 oz.)	soft flour
790 g	(1 lb. 12 oz.)	shortening
1.4 kg	(3 lb. 2 oz.)	sugar
30 g	(1 oz.)	salt
68 g	(2¼ oz.)	baking powder

75 g	(2½ oz.)	milk powder
420 mL	(14 oz.)	cold water
1 kg	(2 lb. 4 oz.)	eggs
225 mL	(8 oz.)	cold water
10 mL	(2 tsp.)	vanilla

Method

1. Carefully measure the ingredients.
2. Grease the cake tins and lightly dust them with flour.
3. Sift the flour and place the first two ingredients in a mixer. Blend together for 5 min at low speed.
4. Scrape down the sides of the bowl.
5. Add the next four ingredients and blend for a further 3 min at low speed.
6. Scrape down the sides of the bowl.
7. Add the 420 mL (14 oz.) of cold water and blend for 2 min at low speed.
8. Scrape down the sides of the bowl.
9. Add the last three ingredients and blend for 2 min at low speed.
10. Scrape down the sides of the bowl. The finished batter should be soft and smooth and pour like a thick sauce.
11. Pour the batter into the cake tins, filling each tin half-full.
12. Bake the cakes in a preheated oven at 190°C (375°F) for 20 min, or until golden brown.

A gentle touch with the finger at the centre of the cakes will indicate if the cakes are done. The centre of the cake should spring back after a gentle touch. If the mark made by the finger remains, it means that the cake is not yet fully baked.

Cakes that are fully baked should be allowed to cool on a rack. They may be removed from the cake tins when they are still slightly warm. Letting a cake cool for a time after removing it from the oven allows the cake to set. A hot cake will crumble if it is removed from the tin too soon. A cake that is allowed to cool completely in the cake tin may become soggy on the bottom. Therefore, it is important to remove the cake from the tin while it is still slightly warm.

This white cake batter can be used for cupcakes, layer cakes and large sheet cakes.

Chocolate Cake

Yield: 6 cakes 25 cm (10 in.) in diameter

960 g	(2 lb. 2 oz.)	soft flour
180 g	(6 oz.)	cocoa
790 g	(1 lb. 12 oz.)	shortening
1.4 kg	(3 lb. 2 oz.)	sugar
30 g	(1 oz.)	salt
30 g	(1 oz.)	baking powder
15 g	(1/2 oz.)	baking soda
90 g	(3 oz.)	milk powder
480 mL	(16 oz.)	cold water
1 kg	(2 lb. 4 oz.)	eggs
300 mL	(10 oz.)	cold water
5 mL	(1 tsp.)	rum flavouring

Method

1. Carefully measure the ingredients.
2. Grease the cake tins and lightly dust them with flour.
3. Sift the flour and cocoa together and place them with the shortening in a mixer.
4. Blend them together for 5 min at low speed.
5. Scrape down the sides of the bowl.
6. Add the next five ingredients and blend them for a further 3 min at low speed.
7. Scrape down the sides of the bowl.
8. Add the 480 mL (16 oz.) of cold water and blend for 2 more min at low speed.
9. Scrape down the sides of the bowl.
10. Add the last three ingredients and blend for a further 2 min at low speed.
11. Scrape down the sides of the bowl.
12. Half-fill each cake tin with the cake batter and bake the cakes in a preheated oven at 190°C (375°F) for 20 min.
13. Test the cakes to see that they are done.

This chocolate cake batter can be used for cupcakes, layer cakes and large sheet cakes.

Buttercream Icing

Approximate yield: to cover 30 15-cm (6-in.) layer cakes

900 g	(2 lb.)	butter
675 g	(1 lb. 8 oz.)	icing sugar
10 mL	(2 tsp.)	vanilla

900 g	(2 lb.)	emulsified shortening
16		eggs
675 g	(1 lb. 8 oz.)	sugar

Method

1. Place the butter, icing sugar and vanilla in a mixer and **cream** together at low speed.
2. Scrape down the sides of the bowl.
3. Add the emulsified shortening and continue to cream the ingredients together at low speed until the mixture is soft and light.
4. Scrape down the sides of the bowl.
5. Whip the eggs with the sugar at high speed in a separate mixing bowl.
6. Gradually add the egg mixture to the creamed mixture and blend them together well at low speed.

Buttercream icing may be flavoured and coloured for use with decorated layer cakes.

cream—blend

a. Apply the icing with a spatula. b. Finish by making swirls in the icing with a spatula or a knife.

Fudge Icing   Approximate yield: to cover 12 dozen cupcakes

450 g	(1 lb.)	chocolate fudge base
2.7 kg	(6 lb.)	icing sugar
150 mL	(5 oz.)	corn syrup
570 mL	(20 oz.)	hot water

Method

1. Place the chocolate fudge base, icing sugar and corn syrup in a mixer and cream together at low speed until the mixture is smooth.
2. Scrape down the sides of the bowl.
3. Add the hot water and blend for 5 min at low speed.

This fudge icing may be used for icing brownies, cupcakes and chocolate cakes.

PIES

Pies are made with either one or two crusts. Pies with just one crust are usually filled with a cream or custard and are topped with whipped cream or meringue. Sometimes a fruit filling is used with one-crust pies. If this is the case, the topping is usually a sweet crumb topping. Pies made with two crusts usually have a fruit filling.

Good pie crust is the **key** to successful pies. Although the pie filling provides most of the flavour, a poorly made pie crust will often ruin a pie. A good pie crust should be tender and crisp with a light brown colour. It should be flaky when broken and the taste should be **delicate**.

RECIPES

Pie Dough   Yield: 6 two-crust pies 20 cm (8 in.) in diameter

900 g	(2 lb.)	soft flour
450 g	(1 lb.)	chilled shortening
15 mL	(1 tbsp.)	salt
300 mL	(10 oz.)	cold water
		eggwash

Method

1. Accurately measure all ingredients.
2. **Sift** the flour into a mixing bowl.
3. Break up the shortening and gently rub it into the flour to form pea-size **nuggets**. Work quickly or the shortening will become too warm. Do not overmix.
4. Dissolve the salt in cold water.
5. Make a well in the flour-and-shortening mixture and pour the cold water into it.
6. Gently fold the water into the flour-and-shortening mixture. Fold gently from the bottom of the mixing bowl to the top. A few folds like this will quickly allow all the water to be absorbed. Do not overmix.

key—something that makes another thing possible

delicate—subtle and pleasing

sift—pass through a fine sieve to remove or break up large particles

nuggets—lumps

Cherry pies (Courtesy of the Ontario Ministry of Agriculture and Food)

The finished pie dough should be slightly sticky, lumpy and medium-soft to the touch. If the dough is too dry, sprinkle a little more water over it and fold gently until the water is absorbed. If the dough is too moist, sprinkle a little more flour over it and fold gently until the flour is absorbed. Once the dough is finished, chill it in the refrigerator before rolling it out.

Making and Baking Two-Crust Pies

1. Lightly grease the pie tins.
2. Place the chilled pie dough on a flour-dusted bench and gently shape it into a ball. Do not knead the dough. Kneading will toughen it.
3. Divide the dough into six equal pieces for six 20 cm (8 in.) pies.
4. Divide each of the six equal pieces into two more pieces. These two pieces should be divided in the ratio of approximately two-thirds to one-third. The larger piece is used for the bottom crust while the smaller piece is used for the top crust.
5. Starting with the **bottom crusts**, flatten each piece of dough on the lightly floured bench. Dust a rolling pin and the top of the dough lightly with flour to prevent sticking.

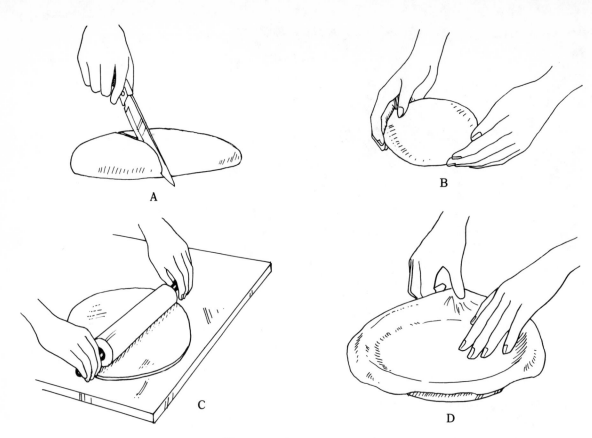

A

B

C

D

How to make a two-crust pie

6. Roll the dough into the shape of a circle that is slightly larger than the top rim of the pie tin. To check this, place the pie tin over the rolled-out dough to see if the dough is large enough to cover the bottom and sides of the pie tin. Be sure to roll the dough to an even thickness (about 3 mm or $\frac{1}{8}$ in.).

7. Fold the dough in half and lift it gently. Place the folded edge in the centre of the pie tin so that one-half of the tin is covered with pie dough. Gently unfold the dough so that the entire pie tin is covered.

8. Gently press the dough against the sides of the pie tin.

9. Brush excess flour from the rim of the pie crust and moisten the rim with eggwash so that the completed pie will be properly sealed.

10. Fill the pie almost to the top with a fruit filling.

11. Roll out the dough for the **top crust** evenly. Make it slightly thinner than the bottom crust. Roll out just enough to cover the top rim of the pie tin.

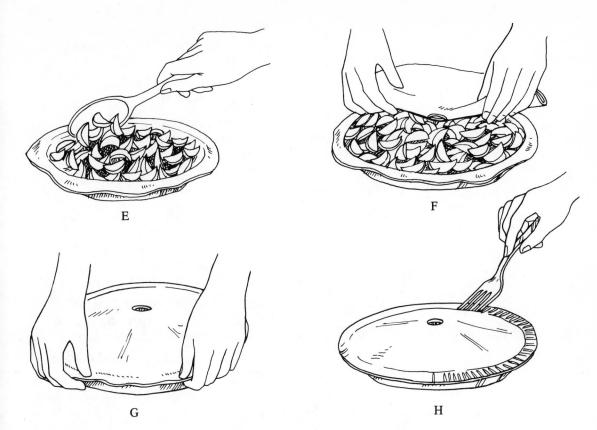

E

F

G

H

12. Make some slits in the dough for the top crust with a sharp knife. This will allow steam to escape while the pie is baking.
13. Fold the dough in half and lift it gently. Place it so that half the pie filling is covered. Unfold the dough to completely cover the pie.
14. Seal the edges of the pie by using your fingers to pinch the edges of the top and bottom crusts firmly together. You may also seal the edges by pressing the **tines** of a fork against the rim of the pie tin.
15. Remove any excess dough by cutting it away from the rim with a sharp knife.
16. Brush the tops of the finished pies with eggwash to ensure a shiny, browned top crust when the pies are baked.
17. Bake at 220°C (425°F) for 30 min.
18. Remove the pies to cool on a rack. Allow the filling to cool and set before serving.

tines—prongs

Making and Baking Single-Crust Pies

For a single-crust pie, use the same amount of chilled pie dough as was used to make the bottom crust of a two-crust pie.

1. Place the chilled pie dough on a flour-dusted bench and gently shape it into a ball. Do not knead the dough.

2. Flatten the dough lightly. Dust a rolling pin and the top of the dough lightly with flour to prevent sticking.

3. Roll the dough out into a circle until the dough is about 6 mm (¼ in.) thick and approximately 2.5 cm (1 in.) larger than the top rim of the pie tin.

4. Grease the back and outside of the pie tin.

5. Fold the dough in half and lift it gently over the back of the pie tin so that the folded edge of the dough is in the centre of the tin and one-half of the pie tin is covered. Gently unfold the pie dough to cover the entire back and outside of the pie tin.

6. Gently press the dough against the outside of the pie tin. This will remove trapped air and prevent any air pockets from forming during baking.

7. Trim the excess dough from the rim of the pie tin with a sharp knife.

8. Puncture the dough on the pie tin in several places with the tines of a fork.

A single-crust apple pie (Courtesy of the Ontario Ministry of Agriculture and Food)

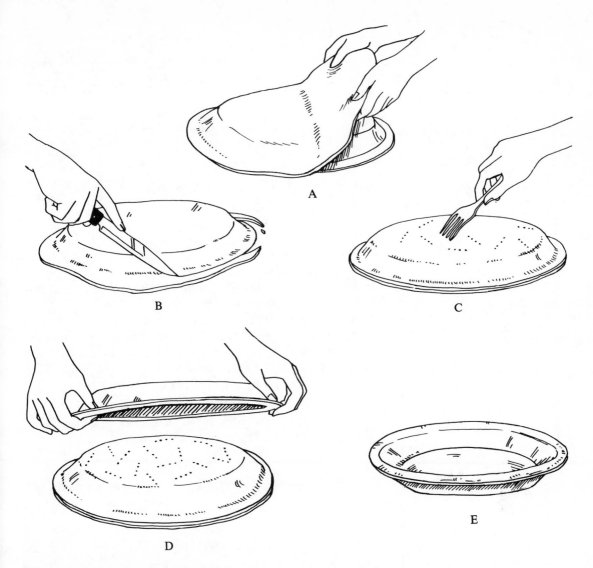

A

B

C

D

E

How to make a single-crust pie

9. Bake the shell at 220°C (425°F) for 20 to 25 min, or until the crust is golden brown.

10. Allow the pie shell to cool before removing it from the back of the pie tin and placing it on the inside of the tin.

This prebaked pie shell may be filled with a variety of precooked fillings such as chocolate, lemon, butter-scotch and coconut fillings. One-crust pies may be topped with meringue or whipped cream.

Short Paste

Approximate yield: 6 20-cm (8-in.)
single pie crusts

900 g	(2 lb.)	shortening or butter
450 g	(1 lb.)	sugar
15 mL	(1 tbsp.)	salt
10 mL	(2 tsp.)	vanilla
2		eggs
60 mL	(2 oz.)	milk
1.4 kg	(3 lb. 2 oz.)	soft flour

Method

1. Place the shortening, sugar, salt and vanilla in a mixer and cream together at low speed.
2. Scrape down the sides of the bowl.
3. Add the eggs and milk while continuing to mix at low speed until thoroughly blended.
4. Scrape down the sides of the bowl.
5. Add the flour gradually while mixing at low speed. Mix for about 2 min, or until the dough is smooth.
6. Scrape down the sides of the bowl.
7. Chill the dough in the refrigerator before using.

Short paste may be used to line pie shells and small fruit tarts. It may also be rolled and cut out as cookies. Bake at 190°C (375°F) until light brown.

Crumb Topping

Approximate yield:
topping for 80 small tarts

450 g	(1 lb.)	butter
900 g	(2 lb.)	brown sugar
450 g	(1 lb.)	shortening
10 mL	(2 tsp.)	vanilla
15 mL	(1 tbsp.)	cinnamon
5 mL	(1 tsp.)	salt
1.8 kg	(4 lb.)	hard flour
10 mL	(2 tsp.)	baking powder

Method

1. Place the butter and brown sugar in a mixing bowl and blend them together until they are soft and smooth.
2. Add the shortening, vanilla, cinnamon and salt. Blend together.

3. Sift the flour and baking powder into the mixing bowl and fold them into the shortening mixture until lumps are formed.
4. Rub the lumps between the palms of your hands until small, pea-size crumbs are formed.

Crumb topping may be used to top one-crust fruit pies or small, individual fruit tarts.

Crumb-topped pie and double-crust pie (Courtesy of the Ontario Ministry of Agriculture and Food)

Find the Answers to These Questions

1. What three factors influence the preparation of successful desserts?
2. What do puff pastry and choux paste have in common?
3. List the three methods of mixing cake batters.
4. How do you determine if a cake is fully baked?
5. What are the characteristics of a good pie crust?
6. What is usually used to top a one-crust fruit pie?

GLOSSARY

À LA GRECQUE A method of cooking vegetables which always includes water or stock, olive oil, lemon juice and seasonings

ANTIPASTO Italian appetizers

APPETIZER A small portion of food served before the meal to stimulate the appetite

ARROWROOT A thickening agent which provides a clearer finished product than cornstarch

BAKING A dry heat method of cooking in the oven

BARBECUE To cook meat or poultry on a spit or rack over hot coals or in the oven and baste them with a highly seasoned sauce

BASTE To pour cooking juices over meat or poultry at regular intervals

BÉCHAMEL A cream or white sauce

BEURRE MANIÉ A thickening agent made from a mixture of blended flour and butter

BISQUE A thick, rich soup

BLANCH To immerse briefly in boiling water and then cool quickly

BOUQUET GARNI Herbs, usually parsley, thyme and bay leaf, tied in a small bag and used for flavouring soups, sauces, stocks and stews

BREADING Dipping food in flour, eggwash and bread crumbs before frying

BRETON Vegetable garnish for consommé; usually a julienne of celery, leeks and onions

BROILING A dry heat method of cooking meat, fish and poultry by direct heat, either over hot coals or under gas flames

BRUNOISE Vegetable garnish cut in small dice for soups

CALORIE A unit of heat measurement used to calculate the amount of heat energy produced by particular foods

CANAPÉ An appetizer, usually bread, toast or a cracker with a savoury spread and garnish

CAPON A castrated male chicken, five to nine months old, suitable for roasting

CARBOHYDRATE A nutrient which provides the body with its main source of energy

CÉLESTINE A garnish for consommé, consisting of julienne of thin crêpes

CHEF The person in full charge of the kitchen and its staff

CHOWDER A thick soup made from shellfish, fish or vegetables

CLARIFICATION The process of making consommé clear and free from impurities

COCKTAIL A chilled fruit or seafood appetizer usually served in stemware

CONSOMMÉ A strong flavoured, clear soup

COURT BOUILLON A mixture of water, vinegar and herbs which is used for poaching fish

CROUTON A small cube of bread, browned in the oven or deep fat fryer and served with soups and salads

DEGLAZE To moisten a roast pan with liquid in order to collect the caramelized drippings

DEMI-GLACE A rich brown sauce derived from a reduction of brown stock and brown sauce

DEVILLED Any food which has been flavoured with a spicy, hot condiment such as tabasco, cayenne, mustard or pepper

DUBARRY A garnish for consommé, consisting of small flowerettes of cooked cauliflower

ESPAGNOLE Basic brown sauce

FLORENTINE With spinach

FONDANT Icing made by boiling sugar and water to the crystallization stage and then whipping it to a creamy consistency

FRICASSEE Lamb, veal or chicken pieces simmered in a liquid and served with sauce made from the liquid

FRITTER Pieces of food coated with thick butter and cooked in a deep fat fryer

GARDE MANGER The cold meat department in a kitchen or the person in charge of the cold meat department

GARNISH Small, edible decorations

GRILLING Cooking on a solid griddle

HORS-D'OEUVRE A hot or cold appetizer generally served before a meal

HYGIENE Cleanliness

JULIENNE Cut in long, thin strips

LIAISON A binding agent used for sauces and made from egg yolks and milk

LEAVENING AGENT An ingredient used to help dough rise during baking; examples are yeast, baking powder and baking soda

MARINATE To soak food in brine or juice in order to change or enrich the flavour

METABOLISM The chemical processes through which the body absorbs food

MIREPOIX A mixture of onions, carrots and celery used for flavouring soups, stocks, sauces and stews

NUTRITION The processes by which food is converted into living body tissue; the science that studies the food you eat and the way your body uses it

PARBOIL To boil and partly cook

PAYSANNE Vegetables cut into regular square shapes

POACHING Cooking in water that bubbles slightly

PRINTANIÈRE Spring vegetables cut in small dice

REDUCTION The process of concentrating a liquid by lengthy simmering

RELISH A selection of chilled, raw vegetables served as an appetizer

ROASTING A dry heat method of cooking in the oven

ROUX Equal parts of flour and fat cooked and used to thicken soups, sauces and gravies

ROYALE A garnish for consommé consisting of baked custard made from cream and eggs

SANITATION The practice of maintaining a healthy environment

SAUTÉ To cook quickly in a small amount of fat

SCALLOPINE Small boneless veal cutlet

SEARING Using intense heat to brown the surface of meat

SIFT To pass dry ingredients through a fine sieve to remove or break up oversize particles

SIMMERING Cooking in liquid that is kept just below the boiling point

SOUS CHEF The person who is second in command in the kitchen

STEAMING Cooking in steam in a covered container

STEWING Cooking by simmering for a long time

STOCK The liquid in which meat, fish, poultry or vegetables have been cooked

VELOUTÉ A thick, creamy white sauce

VITAMIN An element of food which promotes growth and good health

BIBLIOGRAPHY

Amendola, Joseph. THE BAKER'S MANUAL. Ahrens
  Publishing Company, New York, 1960.
Andrews, Helen H. FOOD PREPARATION. McGraw-Hill,
  Toronto, 1967.
Ceserani, Victor and Kinton, Ronald. PRACTICAL COOKERY.
  Edward Arnold, London, 1974.
Folson, LeRoi A. THE PROFESSIONAL CHEF. Cahners Books,
  Boston, 1974.
Haines, Robert G. FOOD PREPARATION FOR HOTELS,
  RESTAURANTS, AND CAFETERIAS. American Technical
  Society, Chicago, 1973.
Harris, Ellen A. and Marsh, Bryan. PROFESSIONAL
  RESTAURANT SERVICE. McGraw-Hill Ryerson, Toronto,
  1980.
Howe, Phyllis S. BASIC NUTRITION IN HEALTH AND
  DISEASE. W. B. Saunders, Philadelphia, 1976.
Kinton, Ronald and Ceserani, Victor. THE THEORY OF
  CATERING. Edward Arnold, London, 1978.
Ray, Mary F. and Lewis, Evelyn J. EXPLORING
  PROFESSIONAL COOKING. Chas. A. Bennett, Peoria,
  Illinois, 1976.
Sultan, William J. ELEMENTARY BAKING. McGraw-Hill, New
  York, 1969.
Villella, Joseph A. THE HOSPITALITY INDUSTRY. McGraw-
  Hill, New York, 1975.
Wattie, Helen P. and Whyte, Elinor D. CANADIAN COOK
  BOOK. McGraw-Hill Ryerson, Toronto, 1977.

INDEX

INDEX TO RECIPES